FIBROMYALGIA

The Invisible Illness, Revealed

Organizer/One of the Authors
Barbara Robbins

ISBN 978-1-63844-030-7 (paperback)
ISBN 978-1-63844-031-4 (digital)

Christian Faith Publishing, Inc.
832 Park Avenue
Meadville, PA 16335
www.christianfaithpublishing.com

Printed in the United States of America

Barbara Robbins & Publisher: Front and Back Cover
Special Contributors: Outside Of Chapter Body
(in order of appearance)
Lyric Strickland: Cover Art/Illustration
Kai Porter: Back Cover Photo
Sarah Ban Breathnach: Back Cover Quote
Dr. W. Pridgen: Foreword
Barbara Robbins: Preface
Dr. B. Gillis: Introduction
Dr. J. Robinson: Support Letter of Hope
Fiona Young: Photo Chapter
Hannah Tanas & Autumn Moulton: Essential Oils Chapter
Ashley Lang & An Anonymous Cannabis Organic Farmer:
CBD/Cannabis/Hemp "Basics" (two views)
P. A. H.: Alternative Tips & Tricks
Jayne Robinson: Questionnaire
Barbara Robbins: Graphs & Summary
Barbara Robbins: Administrator & Book Organizer

Dedications

———— ⁂ ————

Fibromyalgia: The Invisible Illness, Revealed is a book written by members of a global fibromyalgia support group. One of the members thought a book needed to be written in support of recognizing fibromyalgia and advocating for a more educated community and medical environment. Sandra was the person who asked "someone" to organize and write this book. We acknowledge her first. She was in hospice at that time and felt seeing the progress of the book would help her have a more fulfilled life until the end.

The second acknowledgment must be given to a truly inspirational person. During the hardships she faced with her health and family, she never spoke without including the Lord in her message. Thank you, Penny Weaver Rice, for being such a good role model and person!

The contributors from nine different countries continued to offer as much information in their chapters and questionnaires as possible. Their faith in God, optimistic belief in life itself, and small gestures, as simple as a smile, makes each of them remarkable!

Last, we acknowledge our Philippine advocate. Her family, friends, and community do not understand this illness and refuse to believe it exists. Unfortunately, much of the world sees fibromyalgia patients this way.

Please, let's make the world wake up! Fibromyalgia is *real*, *painful*, and this illness *cannot* be neglected anymore!

Contents

Foreword

This story begins with a new patient, seated in an exam room, who is defeated, exhausted, and in pain, who is more often than not, seated alone. A few lucky ones are seated next to a loved one. Other spouses or loved ones are in the car in the parking lot or sitting in the waiting room, unable to listen to another endless list of complaints. Unfortunately, for some, the spouse, or their family, called it quits long ago and are nowhere to be found. The physician enters this exam room and quickly realizes that this is another Fibromyalgia (FM) patient. Instantly, they too feel defeated, as they know all too well, that this is a disease they don't understand and cannot fix. How is it possible that in this day and age, there exists a disease so tragic, that it can destroy one's body and one's family support system and render the medical community helpless?

An important FM epiphany took place in November 2014, when I was scheduled to present my team's research at the Academy of the College of Rheumatology Meeting. My team was the first of four featured presentations on FM. They had scheduled us to start at 3:00 PM and finish at 5:00 PM. Not exactly the most desirable time slot for a presentation. The auditorium seated 300, yet less than 50 were in attendance. (If that wasn't sad enough, most of the attendees were persons associated with one of the four presenting groups.) My presentation went smoothly, too smoothly in fact, as no one cared enough to debate or challenge our findings. You see, we had just taken everything that was 'known' about this disease and turned it *on its head!* Our approach was radically different and our data and outcomes were excellent. Then, with the force of an exploding bomb, it struck me *no one cares about this disease.* Sure, I was an outsider, a surgeon for crying out loud. I reasoned that, perhaps, since I had no rheumatologic pedigree, and since I had not worked in the field long enough to earn their respect, the paltry attendance was justified.

Nope, I realized, *they simply just did not care*, as no new attendees arrived to listen to the other three presenters, and many actually left early, eager to get a jump on the after-conference festivities.

Max Planck, a noted Nobel Laureate, once put it this way: "*A new scientific truth does not triumph by convincing its opponents and making them see the light, but rather because its opponents eventually die and a new generation grows up that is familiar with it.*"

So what useful information have I learned over the last decade caring for FM patients? Most importantly, that still to this day, one-half or more of all physicians don't believe that FM is a real disease. Secondly, that those who realize that FM is a disease have no confidence that they can help their FM patients, so they refer them to a rheumatologist. Disturbingly, except for a handful of saint-like rheumatologists, most would rather not see or treat this disease and have lost hope that a scientific breakthrough is possible anytime soon.

I have learned that FM degrades the body and often destroys the victim's relationships with their friends and family. Up until now, no FDA treatment is reliably effective, and most patients have tried all of the approved drugs and have ultimately quit them due to either substantial side effects or a lack of effectiveness.

There is, however, some hope to be found. Finally, a new theory exists that embraces the newest Central Sensitization Theory as well as the earliest FM researcher's belief that a low-level irritating stimulus results in FM. The recent PRID201 FM study is believed to have demonstrated that there is merit to this theory. Finally, a new treatment targeting a suspected major cause of FM resulted in a significant reduction in not only the pain of FM but also the fatigue and depression as well. Further, the blinded end of trial questionnaire suggested that the IBS, anxiety, headaches, TMJ, and brain fog were also improved by this new treatment.

There is still much work to do; before one can draw any conclusions with certainty. Clinical trials need to be successfully completed before we can prove that it takes a combination of medicines with differing antiviral properties to force an everyday, nociceptive virus to sleep, thus halting the central sensitization that results in the magnified pain of FM. That is quite a mouthful, I know.

Vincent et.al. 2013 declares that there are likely 20 million Americans who are very much like the brave individuals who share their experiences in this important compilation of stories. FM disrupts once normal active, happy, interesting people, ultimately isolating them. Yet this important work of shared experiences lets those similarly afflicted know that they are not alone. Patients need to know, given these latest scientific advances, there is every reason to remain hopeful.

By William Pridgen, MD, FACS

Preface

When I decided to organize the writing of *"Fibromyalgia: The Invisible Illness, Revealed,"* I have to admit I did not know what that would entail. One particular fibromyalgia support group member wanted a book written; she identified the necessity of it; she comprehended that this world needed a voice to support and recognize this illness. And yes having fellow patients in the fibromyalgia support group write it would be the perfect avenue to advocate for a more educated community and medical environment. That seemed as compelling a reason as any to "jump in" and organize this book. So while this was another person's idea, as a member of that support group, I felt a kinship with her and wanted to make this book a reality. I can understand and empathize with so many of the support members life experiences and pain.

Most people would be daunted by the undertaking of such a large project-I, on the other hand, seem to thrive with the challenge. It may be my optimism or sheer unwavered faith, but I know, as I've experienced in the past, if I work on a project and get the wheels in motion, without expectation of any personal gain, I can literally step back and God will develop my vision into something more grand than I could have hoped for.

This has happened two other times in my life.

Once, a senior in college, my project assignment was to develop a new snack food. My instructor told us there was a national competition held by a company in California. She entered all the class projects, hoping one of us would win. My project was indeed chosen and is now a globally recognized snack food. I called the company once, after learning about the development and test marketing of my snack food. I was informed that my professor had signed away any "rights" when she entered the projects. When I explained to the attorney of the company that I was not going to ask for any "profit or recognition," I just wanted to tell them that I would be including the project in my portfolio because I had graduated and was in search of a job (my degree: a BFA in Fine Arts with an emphasis in Graphic Design/Illustration). That snack food was a good item to include. They apparently found this harmless and gave me permission.

The second major project occurred after 9/11. My world, as everyone's, had just changed. I have two sons. One was nine, the other two on that tragic day. My oldest had already left for school, my youngest sat on my lap as my husband came into the room, and we watched the second plane hit the second tower. It still brings me to tears. The twin towers, where my husband and I had gone on our honeymoon, and watched a concert between, had just been attacked.

My nine-year-old was traumatized. He would not sleep in his bed, but next to it on the floor, because he felt safer. He was beside himself with anxiety if I was not "exactly" where I said I'd be standing when he ended his school day. In the car a couple weeks after the horrific event I asked him, as any artist would, if it would help to illustrate his feelings about the attack. He thought it would, and my "Children's Memorial" was born. I contacted the Pentagon (no other memorial had been announced for that site yet). My husband was skeptical, telling me he'd be surprised if I got a response. I answered him with an unwavering "we are all equal, I'll hear back." I did. The Children's Memorial, sponsored by several major companies, grew into workshops that I took to libraries in several states during the following summer. It now rests permanently in the Pentagon.

My professional career extended beyond the knowledge those two projects required. I started working for small businesses and printing houses, culminating my career in the university setting. Using my experience and knowledge of prepress work, I eventually created, designed, and supervised the printing, stopped the presses, made adjustments, and signed off on the publications. I've done it all.

I love working with clients. It is a privilege to create these tangible items, produce a design, logo, publication, or project that can't be completely explained. (The client had an idea, but not the complete thought that needed to be conveyed.) I'd start working, using my creative expertise to select how to express their concept. After thumbnail sketches and questions, I turned it into the logo or design they couldn't visualize. Once they saw the finished product, however, they recognized it as their idea. The illustration or design included the list of thoughts they had originally given me. It's a remarkable feeling to be successful at creating something completely new—visually. Clients often looked at me as if I had read their mind, when all I did was assemble their required elements in a unique way.

This is the goal I want to achieve here. A group of fibromyalgia patients, each with unique stories, came together to write their own personal journey with fibromyalgia, in a single chapter. Pair these chapters with the unique photos included by one author, the special chapters on: Alternative Tips and Tricks, Essential Oils, CBD/Cannabis/Hemp "Basics," and results from a questionnaire filled out by every "in group" book contributor comparing the same statistical parameters with "out of group"/non-contributor fibro patients. Add the research and medical expertise provided by the doctors we were privileged to have included, and you have this book. Please understand producing this book took its toll on us all. Brain fog, pain, technical problems, fatigue, plagued each contributor. The remaining chapters are from the members that, despite their "full plates" of daily life, other illnesses, family problems, exhaustion, and too many other items to mention, simply refused to give up. They are the warriors that fought through all to advocate and speak to you, their family, friends, and especially the medical community. Please give them the dignity they deserve and read this book with an open mind.

That is all they've ever asked—to be heard.

Ensuring this book is widely read and popular enough for the medical community to take notice and become better informed will help all fibromyalgia patients. Spreading the word through your time, talent, and profession is the right thing to do. By choosing to help, YOU will have made the world a better place.

This book was meant to be in the hands of everyone that can benefit from its contents. God pushed me to offer to organize the book, now it has landed in your hands. I know the stories seem few and doubt plagues many who do not feel the anguish of fibromyalgia; however, reading this book and passing it on to others will help all the fibromyalgia patients, their family members, and friends gain better care and understanding. Our hope is to help the newly diagnosed have a brighter future with possible cures! The royalties of this book will be donated exclusively to research and treatment of this disease. Thank you.

By Barbara Robbins
Graphic Designer, Illustrator, Organizer of Book

Introduction

Does Fibromyalgia Really Exist?

For decades there has been a raging debate, chiefly among healthcare professionals, as to whether fibromyalgia is an actual medical disease. Despite the fact that we are now in the 21st century, there remains a sizable number of healthcare professionals who are absolutely convinced that fibromyalgia is nothing more than the subjective representation of disparate symptoms that primarily only afflict middle-aged and elderly men and women. These men and women are classified as anxious, depressed, neurotic, hysterical and hypochondrical, among other degrading adjectives. Indeed, FDA-approved medications for fibromyalgia prey on this set of descriptive terms. They are chiefly antidepressant in origin.

Fibromyalgia is as real, however, as pain, fatigue, numbness, tingling, anxiety, depression, and a lack of mental sharpness. Yet, the negative stigma of having the diagnosis of fibromyalgia persists and it has chiefly been the byproduct of claimed "experts" among whom unscientific, unsubstantiated and bizarre connotations of this disease have been attributed to, such as the outrageous "18 point" tender spots that were the original hallmark of how to diagnose fibromyalgia. There may well be significant economic benefits to members of the health profession and the world of pharmacology to continue to promote fibromyalgia as being an arbitrary, disjointed and unproven set of claims for which no objective substantiation has supposedly ever been discovered. For certain groups, the economics of keeping fibromyalgia a non-disease appears to provide great monetary rewards. Indeed, the current allegation by the American College of Rheumatology that fibromyalgia is "medically benign" is truly a disservice to those who are afflicted with this terrible medical disease. It means that there is a continuing effort to label patients with fibromyalgia as individuals who supposedly cannot have any significantly debilitating or factual manifestations.

But pain is real. The inability to have the stamina to work is real. Yet, the overall picture painted of fibromyalgia patients as individuals who are to not be believed, who are to be shunned and who are portrayed as 21st century "lepers" persists.

Consequently, based upon published studies, the average fibromyalgia patient will waste three to five years and $5,000-$75,000 going from physician to physician as they are put through one "rule-out" test after another in search of a diagnosis. Through the latter process of elimination, the end result tends to be a "shrug of the shoulders" by a cynical medical professional and the concurrent implication that fibromyalgia symptoms are impossible to quantify and qualify and unlikely to be reversed.

In contrast and based upon peer-reviewed and published medical research which was initially accomplished at the University of Illinois College of Medicine at Chicago, Department of Pathology, a method to confirm the diagnosis of fibromyalgia to a test sensitivity/accuracy approaching 99% has been available for years. Indeed, thousands of individuals not merely in the United States but throughout the world have been able to rely on this direct, "rule-in" blood test and learn in a matter of days whether they do indeed have this truly provable and documentable medical disease. Yes, fibromyalgia is a real medical disease. Ask anyone who has it. They are not imagining their pain, their weakness, their "brain fog," etc. Through this confirmable FM/a® fibromyalgia blood test, we can answer the critical questions. Does fibromyalgia exist? Absolutely.

Are there objective, reproducible and confirmable criteria, on which to diagnose fibromyalgia? Unequivocally.

We in the 21st century should no longer be debating the legitimacy of the diagnosis of fibromyalgia. We should stop selling and promoting the "snake oil" medications, supplements and myths. We must fight against the self-promoting fibromyalgia support groups and bloggers which, in reality, all too often receive their financial support from the pharmaceutical industry who desires to maintain the status quo and who fail to inform fibromyalgia patients about the latest research discoveries and the pending treatments. We must avoid the chicanery of those promoting supplements, vitamins, and salves who benefit in a significant fashion due to the positive financial benefits they derive by advocating these alleged "quick fixes." None have any benefit on the body's immune system. The identification of the immune system dysfunction and deficiencies proven to exist in fibromyalgia per the well-substantiated science behind the FM/a® test reveals the basis of this disease. Consequently, the treatment of fibromyalgia must be directed at overcoming these immunologic abnormalities.

Indeed, we are soon to embark upon an FDA-approved direct treatment modality to reverse the immune system pathology that has been identified to occur in fibromyalgia. Concurrently, we are searching for genomic markers, mutations and polymorphisms to explain why fibromyalgia occurs. And the latter is happening without any direct economic benefit in that our efforts for treatment are designed to be provided at no cost. Fibromyalgia patients should not be thwarted in their efforts to achieve medical treatment which has been designed and founded on scientific principles.

Does fibromyalgia exist? Is fibromyalgia an actual medical disease? Does the sun come up every day?

Yes, there are and undoubtedly will continue to be the skeptics. There are not merely those who wrongfully think that because a fibromyalgia patient may look normal, they could not possibly be ill. Unfortunately, there will still be those who subscribe to maintaining the highly profitable "rule-out" method of evaluating a fibromyalgia patient. But they are part of those who continue to believe the earth is flat. We cannot allow them to be the obstacles that prevent identifying what causes fibromyalgia, learning how fibromyalgia exists in the body or in regard to determining pathways to reverse this debilitating disorder. Fibromyalgia patients need to be treated with the same deference, respect and support we give any patient with any medical disease. Fibromyalgia patients deserve dignity, compassion, and empathy.

Yes, fibromyalgia is a medical disease that exists. Anyone who disputes this fact, who refuses to accept the objective and proven

evidence, who fails to appreciate the underlying immunologic disturbances or who promotes hypotheticals and innuendos do not merely
perform a disservice. They are actually doing their utmost to continue the pain, the fatigue, the disability and the incapacity that is
associated with fibromyalgia. However, as science progresses, we have
been and we continue to uncover and overcome their shameless and
unwarranted behavior.

Fortunately, Medicare, Champ VA and numerous health plans
pay the cost of the FM/a® test. They accept the science behind this
disease and this accurate manner to diagnose it.

There is no question that those who demonstrate integrity,
principles and truthfulness will succeed in achieving the scientific
accomplishments which we are attaining and which we will continue
to build upon.

Yes, fibromyalgia is a legitimate medical disease with distinct,
unequivocal and objective pathology.

By Bruce S. Gillis, MD, MPH
Epicgenetics, Inc.
www.fmtest.com

Support Letter of Hope

—— ⌒∕⌒ ——

Science Never Sleeps

Right now, there are 30 trials on ClinicalTrials.gov that focus on fibromyalgia.

These are the trials that are currently recruiting or have yet to recruit members to participate. The total number of trials is really over 300 including those who are no longer taking recruits (i.e., they are in the midst of the study) or have completed it.

Being a microbiologist, myself and a fibromyalgia sufferer, I don't think in terms of cures always the skeptical scientist but I DREAM of cures and cures do come! As I read the titles and the methods of each trial, I find many are just "thin," meaning they are a minimal approach by various groups, some not even related to a university or clinical setting. One is even a health supplement! But as I know all avenues must be explored, and that there are many inventions and discoveries that are accidental, being open-minded is required here. The accidental discoveries do supply the need of a particular sector of the economy, and for us, that would be the medical need, so patience is a necessity. (This brings to mind the accidental discovery of Post-It notes.)

Although patience is needed, be aware that science NEVER sleeps and lately more accelerant seems to be pushing the very research we need, during our lifetime. Fibromyalgia is gaining more credibility as more of the medical community realize that it IS a legitimate illness. I have never witnessed the medical world devote so many talented researchers who, I believe, are on the right track when looking at treatments and possible cures for fibromyalgia.

Speaking again, as a microbiologist, and fibromyalgia sufferer, we can all feel good that there are people who are spending their days (and many, many nights) trying to untie the Gordian knot that is fibromyalgia. They will figure it out. So despair not, my fellow fibromyalgia fighters. We will not be left to live in pain forever.

This book is the exact item that was needed for this time in history. The time that will undoubtedly become known as the time of great advances. It is still a time when many have felt lost and scared, but understanding translated into action has arrived. We will be given the tools that can make ourselves better and whole at last.

By Jayne B. Robinson, PhD

Endorsement

We, the administrators of the book, stand by
every contributor and their unique stories.
These personal experiences chronicle their
journey with fibromyalgia.
Contributors, your courage to share your life experiences with
honesty, however painful or discouraging, is to be commended.
You give hope to others needing your truth. We are so proud of you!
Thank you for making this book a reality!

LIST OF FIBRO CONTRIBUTORS BY PEN NAMES

A Canadian Advocate
A Philippine Advocate
Ann Scollins
Barb Bickford
Barbara Lyn
Barbara Robbins
Chemain
Clara Aimola Keatings
Danielle Amantecatl
Debbie Russell
Doug Kuriger
Eleanor O'Farrell
Emily Hinchcliff
Eugenia Volino

Fiona Young
Jack DeSoto
Jayne Robinson
Lesley King
Lynn Andrews
Lynn Declan
Naomi Wilkie
Nicole
P.A.H.
Penny Weaver Rice
Sahara West
Sharonda
Tamara Everhart Smith
T. H. Tracy

A Letter To The World

By *A Philippine Advocate*

Dear World,

I would like to write you a letter explaining the pain I endure each day. I know you have heard this before and you have heard the cries, prayers, and pleas that others have voiced. *"Why aren't you answering them, or me?"* Fibromyalgia is so hard! You don't realize how I try to "put a face on" and let you (the world) see some happy times! I've learned to act and look good. Yes, years of hearing "But you look so good, you can't hurt that bad" has brainwashed everyone in the world, including the doctors we turn to, hoping they will save us from the pain. Instead, they look at us like you do…try to believe the easy thoughts that no one could suffer daily, forever. These fibro patients must be faking their pain for some reason. *"Why the hell would we do that?"* Pain is not fun, or exciting. Pain robs us of a life of fun, and exciting adventures of which we dream!

World,

You think everyone starts and ends with an even playing field, but you are so wrong! Some of us may have been born lucky, even survived awhile as the rest of the 'normal' population, but something changed our lives—fibro. I believe this illness is a combination of daily exposure to toxins, constant stress and at some point (or many times) trauma. This combination "flipped our switch" and before we realized it our "normal" was gone. We look for it everywhere, seeking out guides (our doctors) to find our old self again. Instead, we become a joke. These guides don't have answers for us, so they treat our illness as being insignificant. *"What did we ever do to deserve your disgust, disbelief, lack of compassion, or your questioning eyes?"*

World,

We never asked for any of our symptoms. You say to us, "There are SO many symptoms" you can't understand how you can help. Okay we, the patients, don't understand either, but we do know one thing that everyone with fibro experiences pain! I look at the world, see the pain caused by natural disasters, automobile accidents, cancer, other "understandable" visible diseases. I want to rid the world of these traumatic events. *"Don't you want to help me get rid of my pain?"*

World,

Why does everything you believe in have to be visible? *"Don't you have faith in anything other than what you can see?"* If you do, how can you dismiss people's cries or pleas for help? Friends and family members tell me I'm lazy. They know I have RA (rheumatoid arthritis), MS (multiple sclerosis), migraines, back problems, and other health issues. I tire easily and can't take care of much more than myself, yet their response is "get more exercise." When I tell these friends I am limited and cannot do more because I'm having trouble taking care of myself they say that can't be so. "You used to do this, or that, you can find time and energy to do those things again."

"When?" I ask. I am either too exhausted, no matter how much I sleep it's not enough. It's like my body aged 30 years overnight. Or I cannot sleep at all due to the stress of worrying about my responsibilities, *"how do I get to my doctor appointments, get my errands done, take care of my home?"* Sleeping two to three hours a night is making me susceptible to developing other illnesses, but the doctors do not help me. Some (well-known doctors) refer me to a pain clinic or a different specialist. I go to make an appointment and they ask what is wrong. I list a couple illnesses, then when I mention fibro, they look at me and say, "We cannot make an appointment for you, we do not treat fibro." Maybe if they saw me, heard my sensitivities, allergies, pain, and other illnesses they would have a recommendation for me, and maybe medicine that I can take. I'm open to alternative therapies, suggestions from other doctors, but it's easier to turn me away.

World,

I am not asking for a handout, I AM asking for a doctor who has enough integrity and character to give me an appointment, steer me away from medicines or therapies that would not benefit me and look at me as an individual. Together, we could find a starting point to eliminate my pain. I'm not asking for too much. Doctors that are reading this, know I'm right. I don't care if you are given only a specific amount of time to see me, make those minutes count! You, the doctor, can make our time together productive. You can choose to help treat me as a family member or discard me because I would be a challenge. But I think you would learn so much from me and my complications, and we could help others! Don't think I'm not loyal, because I am. If you help me by trying to uncover problems, or by trying new ideas, I will spread the word. You will become popular and just maybe, we could save our next generation from developing fibro! "*Wouldn't you like to keep your own children safe from pain?*" At least pain you may be able to reduce? You are right, some pain is unavoidable, but not fibro.

World,

We could wipe fibro off the face of the world. That is the whole point of this book. Thank you, world, for listening.

Book Organizer's Comments

I read the above letter and had to comment.

Do you realize the United States is seen as one of the most progressive countries? Why then is a diagnosis of fibromyalgia not treated equally among all the doctors in this country? How can the United States help other countries see this illness correctly if the professionals here can't even look at an illness the same way? *We can help others around the world only if we are consistent with the patients within our borders.*

I live here. The above letter is not how I am used to being treated. (But when it comes to fibro, as of seven years ago, I am treated as our fibro friend above.) I had a great rheumatologist who had RA herself. She was a kind, empathetic, caring doctor. Her visit with each patient *lasted from half an hour to one and a half hours. She was not a doctor for the establishment or with ambitions to be wealthy. She was a doctor to help people who suffered and needed guidance. She retired seven years ago when we moved away. In seven years, with all the doctors and specialists I've needed for my other illnesses, I have not found one rheumatologist or doctor that cared enough to help me find one good fibro doctor. I have health insurance. I am on disability, but my private insurance is my primary insurance. If you treat a person who has the ability to pay for private insurance poorly, how are others with Medicare, Medicaid, or no insurance treated? It scary to look into the future!*

The "F" Word

By Sahara West

I'd like to introduce myself and tell you who I was. Yes, I said I want to tell you who I was. The fact is that for any of you to understand the difficulty of my current life, you have to know a little bit about me before invisible chronic illness. As most of us with fibromyalgia, I tend to look at everything in what I refer to as "BF" before fibro and "AF" after fibro. In my case I really should say before chronic illness because like many with fibro I have a lot of diagnosis, although I'm not even going to get into all that. Fibro is just the great big rancid cherry on the top of my life sundae.

My name was Sahara and I was awesome. Okay, so I know my name is still Sahara, but I'm trying to make a point. I know I should be more humble but it's true I really was awesome. I was a very active and happy person, even when the circumstances didn't swing in that direction. In high school I loved to skate, and I could twist and jump and do the "Hamel Camel." I enjoyed playing tennis and could run around on the court for hours if I could bribe someone to play with me. I had endless energy and general enthusiasm. I played the clarinet in the band and I loved twirling baton. I was very active. I was never popular in school, but I had plenty of friends and enjoyed just being around myself because I was excellent company. I was smart and well read. I devoured books like each one was the last I'd be able to read. I can't do that today. I have no concentration. I grew up loving dogs and took up breeding and showing them. I would run around the ring with my dogs almost every weekend, just enjoying life. I even bred a few champions back in the day. I was able to pursue my passions and I became a dog groomer, owning several grooming salons along the way.

Things always change as you grow up, that's inevitable, but my life was bumpy for a lot of years. I became a wife and a mom and had to endure a mentally abusive marriage. I continued working as a pet groomer and really enjoyed my job, it was an escape from my trauma filled marriage. Even though the marriage was the worst, I still felt lucky in life, mostly because I didn't dread going to work. I actually missed work when I was away from it for long periods of time. Thankfully my bad relationship came to an end. Life, motherhood and my career moved on. I had so many friends at this point and I was thrilled to be away from my mental abuser and now my life was wonderful!

I eventually met and married a good man who still makes me laugh today. We started our lives together as a new family. I started my own business. Life was good. Then it happened (*dun, dun, dun*) invisible chronic illness. It pretty much arrived like the villain in a super hero movie. It was ugly and evil. It swung in and dragged me off into the night. The me I was, is just gone. She is only a memory to me. She was fearless, fierce, and her fire just went out. I mourn the loss of her every single day. I'm still waiting on the super hero guy to do his job and bring me back, but so far life is not imitating art. Like most with chronic illness the doctors were about as helpful as the nonexistent super hero guy.

Now that you know a little bit about who I was, I feel like the reality of who I am, currently, might have a bigger impact on you. Making that impact is my goal. I was really happy to do this chapter when I first heard about it. I thought it could be a great project to help people understand what we all go through. I will admit I almost backed out when I realized that people I know might read the book. This book is about the truth. This chapter is about my own personal truth. I don't even like to admit that truth to myself, let alone others. To be quite honest, I'd like to draw over my feelings and pain with a big fat sharpie, like one of those classified confidential FBI/CIA files that you see in the movies.

Some things just feel safer when kept locked away. They say the truth sets the soul free, but what if my soul just wants to stay locked away in the closet with a nice audio book, a pillow and a pound of chocolate? Face it, there's safety in a cage. The truth is, we can't all stay locked away in our safe places because if we do we can't change the world. We have to reach down deep inside and find the warrior in each of us.

Change starts with one person and one thought at a time. If I can cause that one person to change their mindset on this awful thing we call fibro, then I have done my part. I can't give you medical information. I can't explain the how and why of this thing. I can only tell you how I feel. I can tell you what it's really like. Trust me when I say that if you do not have it, you do not have a clue what it is like. I will try to keep it real, and share my inner most personal thoughts, which aren't all sunshine and roses so buckle up.

The "F" word, that's what I call it. Try to imagine having this horrible thing that changes your life and you can't even say it by name. Saying the word makes you feel guilty. Saying it makes you feel unworthy. Saying it makes you feel like a crazy person. I know people who hang their head down when they tell someone they have fibro. It's almost like they're telling them they have a STD or something. The amount of ignorance associated with the word is ridiculous, but I can't act high and mighty because I too have rolled my eyes into the back of my head when someone told me they had fibro. Yes, I was awful. I now find myself whispering it to someone, like I'm telling them a deep dark secret. I'm here today to try to educate those of you reading this so that you never make someone feel inferior for having something that they have no control over.

If you're reading this and you have the "F" word then know that you're not alone. I'm right here beside you. Why is this thing called fibro so different than let's say having cancer, heart disease, or MS? Maybe it's because the "F" word isn't fatal. Fatal or not, the fact is that none of us signed up for this thing. Trust me when I say that I didn't want to lose almost everything that made me, me. From now on I will try not to hold my head down and whisper in shame like I've done something wrong or like I'm a mental case who is just seeking drugs and/or attention. That's what I fear people think of me. Let me tell you though that I don't want either of those things.

I want acknowledgment that what I have is a real thing and that I'm not just depressed.

Let's talk a little bit about the preconceived notions people have about us. People think we are faking it. Guess what, they are right. We are faking it. They think we are faking being sick when in reality we fake being well almost every single day. We feel like we have to fake being well because we can't admit how bad we feel all the time. We fear we might lose all the people around us because nobody wants to hear it. This is just one thing we deal with on a daily basis. It isn't such a big deal when attitude comes from strangers or so called friends but it does hurt when it's your family or good friends. I'm tired of hearing the word, "Oh?" Yes, that's what I said. I tell someone I'm not feeling up to doing something like driving, walking or shopping and the response is, "Oh?" said with a questionable "tone" or "Okay" said with annoyance. I really hate those words. What's worse is when they say nothing at all. Maybe they just don't know what to say or they don't want to say anything more meaningful because then they might have to have a real conversation about why you're not feeling up to said thing you were supposed to do that day. I don't have to be looking at them to see the annoyance and disbelief on their faces. Don't think that you're sly in hiding your true feelings, I can sense it all the way on the other side of the room. I see in my mind's eye the "frown," the "eye roll," and the "furrowing of your brow." I will admit I'm extra sensitive to the way I feel I'm being perceived by others, so perhaps some of it is in my head. I know I'm a little crazy, so therefore I'm not truly crazy at all. Isn't that what they say?

When it comes to my husband, he just doesn't seem to get it. I don't know if he doesn't believe me or just doesn't want to admit to himself that I'm not the same woman he married. Maybe he thinks I'm faking it or it's because I need to lose weight. It's very hard for me to admit that I'm unable to do something. When I say I can't do something all the talking points in the world won't change that. I still cannot do it. Think about it for a minute. I was super woman. I have single handedly carried an entire trunk full of groceries into the house in one swoop, just because I could. These days, I just can't. With each of those little loses I die a little bit more inside. I shrivel and shrink away into nothingness. When my husband asks me to do something simple and I have to say no, it's hurtful getting the words out. It hurts me because I don't know if he thinks I'm just trying to get out of something or if he's angry. I can understand his anger, I'm angry too. Anger is an emotion I have to deal with just about every day. I am so angry at myself because I don't like being that person that disappoints the people who are counting on me. On the outside I may be mellow but on the inside I'm crying every time I let you down. My self-loathing grows a little more with every passing day. It's very easy to get down and stop caring about ones' health at all. There are days I just want it to be over. Next please.

I think by now you are getting the idea that the worse thing about fibro for me isn't the physical pain of it, but the mental aftermath of having such constant pain. When you've lived your life for 20, 30, 40, or 50 years acting and being a certain way, that *way* becomes what's expected of you. When you have to stand back and take a look at your life and your new limitations, it's beyond just being hard. It's literally mentally exhausting.

Another of my daily emotions is guilt. My guilt is horrible. My husband is a hard worker and when I see that he is working his off days and his holidays in order to cover for my new shortcomings, I feel worthless, less than a big fat zero. I know all about that whole, for better or worse thing, but the reality is that marriage is a contract and I feel like I'm not fulfilling my end of it. I shouldn't be his burden to carry through life, the proverbial albatross. Who wants to be an albatross? There's such a deep hurt when you know your very existence is causing someone else pain and anxiety.

I'm not suicidal, please understand that, but I get how people can arrive there at that horrible place. My beliefs tell me that God gave me my life and every day is a gift from him. He didn't have to allow me to wake up this morning, but he did. Many people were not that lucky. That in itself keeps me moving forward, but there are times when thinking of death brings a wave of inner peace to me. Just the fact that the worry and pain would be over, and that's a scary cliff to be balancing on. There are days when that fight instinct switches to flight and I just want to run. I want to run away from everyone I'm hurting, everyone I'm letting down, I want to run away from myself. I guess, for me, these occasions usually happen when I have about $50 in the bank so I wouldn't get much farther than the snack isle of the gas station. I'm still here battling like the rest of the fibro warrior squad, trying to kick pain and anxiety's ass. Some days I'm the windshield but most days I'm the bug. I feel like the iconic snake, eating its own tail most of the time. Anxiety leads to a lack of sleep which leads to physical pain which leads to no productivity which leads me back to anxiety. Yeah, that's me, that's my problem. Don't mind me. There's nothing to see here; just eating my own tail. Just a day in my fibro life.

I've so far avoided the whole talking about constant pain thing. I guess I'd rather talk about my mental struggle than the actual physical ones. I'm not sure why but it makes me feel weak to talk about my pain. The whole point in writing this chapter is to talk about that pain, so here we have it. When I wake up in the mornings the first thing I feel is nausea. I've felt it every day since long before I was diagnosed with fibro. I had never heard of fibro causing this but yet I've spoken with others who have the same symptom, so I'm blaming it on the "F" word, even though my doctor isn't convinced it has anything to do with it. There are days I have just simple nausea and days when I have full blown vertigo which brings on a different kind of nausea all together. If it's a day I need to actually get up at a certain time then I have to set several alarms. The fatigue is real. It takes a while to feel like I can get out of bed without throwing up, especially if the room is spinning that day. My hands don't work in the morning, my fingers feel like big fat sausage links and using them is near impossible. It hurts so bad to bend them. A couple fingers are usually triggered in the morning. If your unfamiliar with the term it means that the tendon sheath is so inflamed that the tendon can't pass through smoothly. Before you say anything, yes, I'm on an anti-inflammatory diet or at least I try to be, but I still have inflammation.

After about 30 minutes I'm usually stable enough to force myself to get up. Sitting on the side of the bed my hip hurts and my right leg is generally numb. I have a torn meniscus in my right knee as well as a fractured right foot that didn't heal properly, so the whole right side of my body is screaming at me to just get back in the bed. I stumble around trying to put most of my weight, which is way too high, onto my left side. My left ankle is weak and feels like it's going to give. I feel a little bit like a troll hunched over and favoring one side as I shuffle along most mornings. Once I finally make it up, my brain doesn't function for a good hour. I sit on the couch like a zombie. I can't eat because I'd be sick if I even tried. I pretend to occupy myself with my phone but I'm really too foggy to know what I'm looking at. My body aches like I'm coming down with the flu. My thigh muscles and calf muscles are burning just from the walk into the living room. Once I sit, the first muscle cramp usually hits. I have to rub my calf as hard as I can to work the knots out.

When my husband is home, he is so perky in the mornings I just want to throat punch him. I don't because it would take energy and strength that I do not have. I'm kind of, maybe kidding, just a little bit, I do enjoy watching him make his coffee and listening as he sings me a stupid song. I'm maybe a little bit jealous that I can't find the same enthusiasm as he has to start my day. He says he's just trying to wake up, and I'm thinking ugh, why do you want to do that. Still, he is priceless entertainment that I'm thankful for. I usually sit on the couch for several minutes and just access my current condition. This might sound odd but every day is different and each day has its own struggles. Today I woke up with a mostly clear head which is why I chose today to get some writing done. I never know what tomorrow may bring. Some days I can't manage to read simple instructions, let alone write down my thoughts.

I'm not going to get into all my aches and pains because there's only so many pages in a proper chapter. I'm just going to talk about today. Today I have costochondritis pain. This is an inflammation of the cartilage that connects our ribs to our breastbone. This is very common for those that suffer with fibro. I have this almost every day, although it's supposed to be treatable and only last a few days to a few weeks, but that's not the case for me. I'm always so special. My costochondritis is what they call chronic, meaning that I have it to some degree most of the time. My chest and ribs hurt if you touch them, and they hurt if you don't touch them. Some days I feel like an elephant is sitting on my chest. Today I feel more like I have an anaconda wrapped around me and he is squeezing. It's difficult to breathe deeply and I hear myself wheezing. My ribs feel like they are broken or like what I assume a broken rib to feel like. It's definitely a no bra kind of day. I sit here typing with my numb leg and my broken back and ribs, feeling like I am having a heart attack, but knowing that I'm not. This pain is just the costochondritis.

The funny thing is I'm still thinking what a great day this is, because I'm mentally clear for the first time in a long while. Sometimes I don't realize how bad off I am until I have a good day or one of my many symptoms disappears for a bit. When this phenomenon happens, I usually clean like a mad woman on a mission, or take care of bills or other things that on most days seem too daunting to attempt. I have to take advantage of these good days when I don't feel quite as "broken" as I'm used to feeling. I'm so thankful for the clarity of mind today, to tell you about my aches and pains.

My wrist is swollen and becoming more painful as I type and I have to take breaks here and there because my back can't handle sitting in this upright chair for more than 15 minutes at a time. I also have sciatica and it's a mean little bitch. My neck and my good shoulder hurt today. I hate it when the good shoulder hurts because I'm not accustomed to that pain.

When we have pain for long periods of time we get used to it and grow to accept it as a part of us, but a new pain is always the worst thing. I think we put up mental and emotional walls and are able to put up walls for some of our physical pains and I haven't yet constructed one for my good shoulder. I hope this doesn't become a constant thing because I don't want to put the time and pain into building that wall.

One of the things bothering me today is what I call a "phantom itch." Imagine having fleas but you get no relief from scratching. That's one of my issues today. I feel like there are tiny things crawling on my scalp. There is nothing there, it's just the creepy crawlies. You can scratch and it might feel better for about two seconds but then it's back. I'm very lucky that this doesn't happen to me often because

I feel like it might drive me over the edge completely. My new doctor says it's a nerve condition that's common with both fibro and MS patients. My old doctors told me it was probably just in my head and I should take a "chill pill." No, it's ON my head, not IN my head. This is why we are untrusting of doctors.

I've taken a little break because my muscles were cramping up. Thank goodness for muscle relaxers because I don't know how I'd function some days without them. These are the only thing I take to help me cope with my fibro, although I think that might have to change soon. Well, I say that, but in reality I'm not real certain I'll even have the muscle relaxers for much longer. The problem many of us have is that we just don't have money anymore. Nobody wants to talk or tell strangers about their financial situation but it's a part of this thing we call fibro. *It's a big part.* I went from working 40+ hours a week down to working about 30 hours, but accomplishing only 20 hours' worth in that time. I had to sell my business because I couldn't physically or mentally cope. I was no longer making any money. Currently, I work maybe two or three hours a week or less from home. My life is so different from what it's supposed to be. Like I said earlier, I didn't sign up for this shit. They weren't kidding when they said if you want to make God laugh just tell Him your plans. The universe it seems didn't get my memo entitled "Sahara's Life Plans."

I have several doctors that I'm supposed to see every six months but how do you do that? I am lucky to have insurance but there are still co-pays to come up with and medication to buy. Let's not even talk about the cost of lab work! I used to take supplements that really helped, but I can no longer afford a few hundred dollars every couple months for supplements. I can't even afford my Thyroid and Sjogren's Syndrome medications. It leaves me feeling so hopeless. Life is a big catch-22.

I need to quit working altogether, but how does one do that? How do I quit working and afford to go to the doctor. You can't work and get approved for disability, but you have to be seeing your doctors and be up to date on your medications to get disability. Do you see my problem? I have a husband that is a good provider, he pays all the bills. I contribute where I can or at least I used to. I have nothing to contribute anymore. He is doing his best to be debt free so he can retire and I just keep ruining his plan every time I need money for something. I skip the medications and I skip the doctor's appointments and the supplements. I skip the healthy foods and I just keep going trying to work when I can. The fact is, a lot of us are still working by sheer grit and determination. It's amazing the things we can force our body to do when we just feel like there's no other option.

Every day myself and millions like me get up, put one foot in front of the other and we just do it. It's sad that there's not a better understanding of this thing. It's sad that there's not an easier way for people who have worked their entire lives to get the disability they paid into and deserve. It makes me so angry and I have no idea what to do or how to keep going or how to even deal with this anger.

There are so many roads to choose from and quite frankly, they all suck. I think to myself, if my family and friends don't really believe there's anything wrong with me, why would the social security administration? They don't even know me. The fact is that you haven't walked in my shoes. Trust me I'd be more than happy to let you try them on for size for a day or two. The nice people say how they wouldn't wish this thing called fibro on their worst enemy. I'm a Scorpio, so I would wish this bitch on every last one of you for a day, only then would you really know what it's like. It would change everybody's perception of us. They would learn the word empathy one hour and one ache and one pain at a time. They would no longer minimize our pain. They would no longer say, "Oh yeah, I've had that," every time we mention a hurt. No, no you haven't. When I say I'm having muscle cramps don't pretend you even know a thing about it until your calf muscle tightens up so tight you feel like your bone is going to break you then just don't know. You don't know about muscle twitches until your thumb is twitching so badly that you can't hold a fork to eat or a cup to take a drink. When you do this thing that you do, trying to make it sound like you have the same aches and pains as we do, what we are hearing from you is that our pain isn't important. We hear that our pain is normal and we should just move on and not talk about it. We just want to be validated. I just want to be validated. I don't want to feel like everyone around me thinks I'm 'faking it' or that I just 'can't accept' that I'm growing old. I'm not having growing old pains I'm having fibro pain. Why can't the world see this? Am I fat, yes, I am. Am I having fat pains? No, I am not. I'm having fibro pain. Losing weight is not going to stop this nerve pain. Losing weight is not going to stop the "brain fog" that caused me to fly straight past a school bus with its *stop* arm out or getting lost in a town that I've lived in for 15 years. I hate to be the bearer of bad news but this isn't a pissing contest. This is my life.

When I let my wall down enough to share something that's bothering me, the correct response isn't, "Oh, I have that too." A good response might be "I'm sorry to hear that" or "I'm sure it's scary for you." You could inquire as to how long it's been happening or if I'm still in pain. You could ask if I've spoken to my doctor about it. There are a lot of things you could say in response, but don't say, "Oh, I have that too." I know what that's like. Every time you guys do that, you are trying to diminish what we are feeling. You're trying to normalize something that isn't normal at all. You are making us feel less than you, again. You are basically saying to us that we are just weak and can't handle pain and you are bored with us talking to you about it. Wow, look at that, I answered my own question from earlier, as to not knowing why I feel weak when I speak about my pain. I'm honestly shocked right now. I feel weak because everyone around me makes me feel that way. I guess if I haven't helped anyone else out with this chapter I've answered a question or two for myself. I'm hoping that these chapters put together by myself and others like me can help people find it in themselves to give their loved ones the validation that they seek. We are not after sympathy, just empathy and understanding. We all know that you guys can't fix it and we aren't asking you to. If you can put yourself in our place emotionally, maybe we can understand each other better. Maybe we can all communicate more effectively and with more care and concern. That's my hope. When all else fails, hope is the light at the end of the tunnel. Hope is the ONLY thing most of us broken sufferers have left.

My Voice:
The Struggle To Be Diagnosed

By P.A.H., *Norway*

When I was 13 years old I had my first experience with pain in my joints. I played volleyball at the time, the only activity my parents could afford, and I hit the ball in a strange way that almost sprained my wrist on my right hand. I also landed badly on my right ankle while jumping up to block a ball. I went to the school nurse about my ankle and wrist. I was told I had inflammation in my tendon, so she wanted me to take it easy for two to three weeks. My ankle, although slightly swollen, was found to have nothing wrong with it.

Since then I have had struggles with both and it spread to my other side after a while. When I told my teachers that the school nurse told me to take it easy, the teachers said, well the school nurses don't always know what they are talking about and ignored the recommendations. My parents just said well it didn't hurt before, so why should it now, and ignored it completely. To add to my story, before 13 I had experienced quite a few years of bullying at school, and had parents who did not show much affection, but were really good at giving jobs and chores to do around the house. I had tried to tell them about the bullying, but they did not listen when I talked. By this time, I felt much like a spare mum to my younger sister. I had a general feeling of not meaning anything positive for anyone in this world. However not being believed about the pain was the worst.

A few months after the first pain experiences, my lower back started acting up. The pain was so bad I felt like I could faint every evening when I went to bed, but of course I didn't. After a good while trying to explain this pain to my parents they finally took me to a doctor. My family doctor could not find anything wrong with my

41

back, except that my spine was curved a little bit more than normal, he thought I had a problem with one foot being longer than the other. I was sent to a specialist for my back pains and they found I had one foot about four millimeters longer. I was given an insole to have in one of my shoes and I wore it for a while. It was only the first few weeks I felt a bit better after those weeks the insole was just annoying and did nothing. I stopped wearing the insole without any difference to my back. The looks I got from the doctors and the attitude the people around gave me when I told them I was hurting was the look that said, "She is just saying this for sympathy and it is not true, she is full of lies. She just wants attention." So I went silent.

My parents had a room in the basement across from mine that they rented out. When I was 16, a girl with a dog was renting the room. She was nine years older than me and she became my first long-term friend, outside of school. She wanted to dance swing and asked if I wanted to come too. I explained about my parents not really letting me go anywhere and not having money to let me do so. She told me she would talk to my parents. She did, and I was given permission to go swing dancing with her, as long as she was with me at all times. I loved dancing. I ended up spending quite a bit of time there because it became my free place, the place where I felt I could start finding out who I was.

To add to my story, a few years later I started getting allergies. I had never had allergies before, so my parents certainly did not believe when I started reacting to different things, for example to pollen. I didn't even get sent to the doctors for testing. When I turned 18 and was on my own, the tests showed I did indeed have allergies, but still, no one at home believed me. (I didn't have allergies before so the test had to be incorrect. I couldn't develop allergies as I got older. You were born with them.) In the meantime, my back settled down but I started getting shoulder and neck pains and one of my knees started to act up. These pains were bad enough to bother me, after all I was now getting used to living with pain, but no one believed me. I managed to leave home for a year at the age of 18. It was only about 1.5 hours away from where my parents lived, but at least I didn't have to be at home during the week. I must admit it was a struggle because I did not know me, my limits, my feelings, or anything else. I started to find my voice and speak my thoughts and I ended up as the leader of the student council for the school I attended.

Money was tight in college. I had to move back home when the school year was done. I went home to do swing dancing on the weekends since this was a big thing for me. I had gotten a part time job in a food shop and I wanted to keep the tiniest income I had to myself. Things did not exactly improve at home because of my year away. It was as if I had never left. At 23 I moved to a different city to go to the university. Finally, I had moved away from home, for good. Where I moved I had a doctor who listened when I talked and tried his best to find out what was wrong. He was a student doctor and we only got as far as starting the round of X-rays of my knees and found that I, now, also had asthma. He suggested that a rheumatic illness of some sort was my problem before he had finished his internship and moved on.

By this time, my right knee had acted up so much I had periods where I could not walk on it. The intern doctor managed to write me a letter to the university telling them I could not do exams by hand. I had to use a PC and get extra time due to allergies and pain in my wrist. At least that did help some. By this age I also started to experience fatigue. Every day after school was finished I had to sleep before I could cook and study or before being active in the student environment. I got into a routine of going to my dorm after school, sleep, eat, and then be social (to the best of my ability). Then I'd go back to do more sleeping. I had a good bed but regardless of the quality mattress my back wasn't happy.

A few years later, I had moved back to my hometown and I met my ex-husband. This time I found a doctor who believed in me. I had stopped thinking anyone would listen to my pain and struggles. She took my allergies seriously and she also listened to me when I talked. When I got pregnant with my first child, she took care of me. I had stopped dancing by now because my ex-husband got jealous when I danced with other men. By this time, I was not allowed to go to the doctor alone my ex-husband had to come. He started coming to be part of the follow up on the baby and the pregnancy. In time it became clear that he was going to be with me in *all* my appointments. The pregnancy was ok but I had morning sickness. I did not experience too much pain but at the end I did develop pelvic issues. None were as bad as my pains have been, but enough that I was not allowed to go back to work. During the pregnancy, I also somehow developed an allergy to alcohol. Not that I ever drank much, but now I could not drink anything. When the pregnancy was over, my pains were back. These pains disappeared behind having a beautiful little baby and a husband that was mentally, sexually and emotionally abusive. I could not have focused on anything about my pains by then because I had to protect my baby from her father. She should be happy and he didn't seem to care about her anyway.

My pain increased and a few years after my baby girl was born I had worked up the courage to walk out of my marriage with my little girl beside me. Even though being a single mum with pain and fatigue was not easy, I found a way to manage. I was still working 100 percent and pushing on everything I had to make our days go around so my daughter was happy and healthy. Night sleep was getting worse. (I was really starting to notice that REM sleep was not in the cards for me but I still managed.) After several years of moving around and settling down, I finally found my current husband. I told him at the beginning of our relationship that I might have a rheumatic illness but my goal was not to give up on life because of it. I told him of some of my pain and fatigue struggles but right there and then I was floating on being in love.

I also had an appointment with the local hospital's rheumatologist. She was obviously not interested in helping. She did not listen to what I said, she found excuses for everything I explained. If I told her about my ankle, it was not rheumatic related, it was because I had not been in therapy after the injury, my wrist was because I had not had it still for the period I was supposed to, my back was because I did not wear my insoles. I told her the insoles had no effect and made no difference. She did not listen. I told her how many times I had problems with my wrist or ankle, and what I did to be still with it when I had problems. Nothing helped my pain, or her indifference. Swing dancing actively, up to six hours a week since the age of

16 until I met my ex-husband—meant nothing to the doctor. She did not want to listen. She ended our relationship by sending me off without an explanation. I was now 34 years old. My then boyfriend (now husband), was with me at this appointment and was frustrated on my behalf. Everything working towards a potential diagnose came to a full stop. I have had two pregnancies with my current husband. The first pregnancy was not good. I had an extreme case of morning sickness for the first five months and was bedridden because of it. It moved on to being pelvis problems throughout the rest of the pregnancy, so working was out of the question. My pain was not very bad, but it made itself apparent. Our beautiful baby would only accept mummy as a caregiver, she refused food from anyone else. She did not sleep a lot, and when she did it was a ten-minute power nap. Naturally both my husband and I struggling with exhaustion due to this. Yet again my pain was put aside to take care of our beautiful baby. My husband, who had been without a job for the last two years, got a job in a different town so we had to move. When I got pregnant a second time, I made the first contact with my new doctor in the new place. For me, it was meant to be a general appointment with some of my medical history, my pain, fatigue, and I thought the rest of the appointment would concentrate on the pregnancy. When I was in with the doctor she did the routine first checkup but all she was really interested in was my previous pregnancies and how they were. She did not want to listen. When I told her that I could feel pelvis issues again she immediately put me on sick leave. I was trying to ask if the pelvis issues could come from the pains I have had since I was 13 or if they had to be pregnancy related. She did not listen. I changed doctors after that.

The new doctor was a man. I did not really like having a male doctor. (But there was a female doctor at his office too, she did the exams.) This man is the best doctor I have ever had. During the pregnancy, I finally got diagnosed with birth anxiety. None of the other doctors had listened when I talked about my fears for giving birth. I did not have it the first time around, because I did not know what a birth really was. I did get it after the first birth because the baby was stuck in my pelvis and I struggled a lot to get her out. The second time I gave birth I went to the hospital because of Braxton Hicks contractions. I never had them the first time around so I thought the birth had started. The midwife I met the first time around checked me and told me nothing was started so I could go home. I asked what it was I experienced, and she explained about Braxton Hicks. I asked the midwives, "When will I know the birth has started?"

They answered, "You will know." The Braxton Hicks only got worse, and again, I thought it was the birth starting. The midwife I met this time was telling me off for wasting their time because everything was full. As to when the birth should start I had the same answer. I decided I was not going back too early ever again. This resulted in me almost giving birth in the parking lot on the way to the hospital. The hospital was not impressed with why I came so late. I tried explaining I have no regular time between the contractions, so it was difficult to know what they were and about my experience coming in too early. My third birth was more like my first, without the Braxton Hicks and when I was going into the hospital they were prepared for meeting my needs. I asked for an epidural up front since I had no drugs with the last birth. When I came in they were calm and ready with everything. I had 6 cm opening and they said we have lots of time yet. I was told the anesthesiologist had to go for an emergency before he came to see me. I turned to my husband and said I will not have any then. The midwife was with us all through the birth, and she was shocked to see how right I was and how quickly it all went. Within 30 minutes of arriving at the hospital we had a beautiful baby boy. When my third pregnancy was done, my doctor left to becoming a specialist within general medicine. The temp did not listen when I asked for help to get past the pelvis issues I had during the pregnancy. Even seven months after the pregnancy was done, she would not listen. When my doctor was back from his leave I was so happy. He listened to all my issues, he heard what I told him about the other doctor's answers and explanations for me and my health issues. He told me straight out that these things are excuses and would not explain any of the things that I was having problems with. That the doctors could blame one foot being longer than the other was not even close to being true, because it had been proven that most people have this. A human being is not symmetrically built. At that point I decided to tell him about all of my issues with pain and fatigue, he sent me straight to a new rheumatologist. The rheumatologist listened to me, poked and prodded me, and he believed me. Finally! I got my fibro diagnosis at the age of 37.

My current doctor is awesome. He is someone who has my back and understands. The month after this I asked to get sent to a hearing specialist because I knew something was wrong. I had a problem with my ear that would not clear up alone or with drugs. I was told I needed hearing aids. In all likelihood I had needed them for quite a few years due to nerve damage in both ears. This was five years ago. I am really happy I finally found a doctor who listens. After arguing with my body for five years now, I have finally accepted that disability is what I need to apply for. My body cannot handle being a mum and working on the side. My fatigue and pain are so bad I can't work outside of our home at all.

Ireland, You Are Letting Us Down

꧁

By Eleanor O'Farrell, *Ireland*

My name is Eleanor. I am 41 years old. I live in Bray, Co. Wicklow in Ireland. I was diagnosed with fibromyalgia approximately six years ago and lived with it for over 20 years before my diagnosis. I was in and out of my doctors' office with various vague complaints, aches and pains, and what felt like frequent kidney infections.

Everything came to a head when my partner (now husband) Ronan and I went on holiday to the Cinque Terre region in Italy. These are five coastal towns that are linked by a network of trails. The idea is that you walk to each of them along the stunning coastline. The trails are very rugged and involve a fair bit of climbing up and down steps and hills. We started in the village of Monterosso and walked to the first town, Vernazza. *It nearly killed me!* The pain in my lower calves was indescribable. As I said, it is rough terrain but elderly people were passing us. It's not *that* difficult, but I just couldn't cope with the extreme pain. We had to abort our walking at Vernazza and for the rest of the holiday, I had spasms and pain and could only walk with a pronounced limp. This made me realize that enough was enough when we returned home, I decided I was going to a new GP. I found one in my local town and made an appointment. I explained to her that I had been suffering from different aches and pains, along with fatigue for many years. *During this time, I felt no one would listen or believe me.* My new doctor immediately sent me for blood tests. They came back showing positive ANAs (Antinuclear Antibodies). This was enough for her to send me to a rheumatologist who then diagnosed me with fibro. I feel very lucky that the blood tests showed positive ANAs because this is not an indicator of fibro, but it is what got me to the rheumatologist and lead me to my diagnosis.

The rheumatologist prescribed the antidepressants Amitriptyline and Cymbalta and at first my pain was much improved. Over time, however, I started having flares again and my fatigue was becoming very debilitating. I returned to the rheumatologist but he told me that there was nothing else he could do for me other than to refer me for rehabilitation at a local Hospice. Three weeks passed and I had heard nothing from the Hospice. I phoned and was told that there was a waiting list and that because I had private health insurance, the wait would be longer because they look after the public patients first. This whole time I was on sick leave from work. I ended up being on leave for six months! I still had not heard back from anyone regarding my rehabilitation.

Then, happily, I got pregnant. Suddenly I was well. *I felt amazing!* So I went back to work, and as far as I remember I didn't take one single sick day until my maternity leave. *I have never felt better in my life.* Our beautiful daughter Eliza was born on October 14, 2014. She arrived one month early, and it was a complicated birth due to my retaining the entire placenta. I was sent to surgery immediately after she was born but the team was unable to remove the placenta. I was kept in the hospital for over a week while they tried to decide the best course of action. Finally, I was allowed to go home but informed that I would have to return to the hospital twice a week to be evaluated (there was concern because if an infection set in it could be very serious and even cause my death).

At the time I was dealing with this, Ronan was dealing with our little Eliza, who was born with bilateral talipes (club-foot in both feet). The day after she was born, she was whisked off to the Children's Hospital where they put both her legs in plaster from her hips down. She had to return to the hospital every week to have the plaster changed and her progress checked. So every week, I had to go into the Maternity Hospital twice and the Children's Hospital once. I live about 20 km away from Dublin City Center which is where both of the hospitals are located. This meant that I was driving into the city three times a week, with a very young baby in tow. I was so unwell that a couple of times I almost fainted while I was with Eliza at her check-up. I used to wake at night and be shivering so violently the bed would shake. In fact, I didn't realize how unwell the retained placenta was making me, until after they removed it. (Six weeks after I gave birth, I returned to the hospital to have an operation to remove the placenta.) They had decided to go in through an opening in my stomach; the doctors felt this was the least dangerous option and may save my womb while not risking my life. The placenta had lodged itself into a corner of my (bicornuate) uterus and there was a chance that the uterus wall would rupture. When I woke up from the operation I was told the doctors had decided to try the old fashioned way and this time managed to remove all but a tiny amount of the placenta. They felt this was sufficient and I was discharged feeling much better!

Gradually, my aches, pains, and fatigue returned. As much as I adored being at home with my gorgeous little baby, I found looking after her extremely tiring. I felt like such a failure as a mother because I couldn't handle looking after my girl. It's been four years now and I still feel like a failure at times. Some days, particularly on weekends, I am absolutely exhausted and I suffer from extreme anxiety. My poor husband and daughter bear the brunt of my inabilities and I snap at them, then cry my eyes out. *I feel that I just can't cope and can't imagine how I can continue.* (These thoughts only occur when I am severely agitated because I don't know how to make it stop.) I know how lucky I am. I know that I have an amazing life, with an incredible husband and a miraculous daughter, I just wish I could *show* them!

On good days, I am the happiest girl in the world. I would love to be able to walk along with Ronan, with Eliza in the middle, holding both our hands and swinging her into the air. Unfortunately, most days I can't cope with her pulling on me. *It makes me want to scream.* At the end of a long day, she wants to play hide and seek and I'm at the "crumple and fold" level of tiredness. I just can't. It's awful. I want her to be happy and I want to do everything for her. The sound of her laughter is the best sound in the world and I hate letting her down.

One of the hardest things to deal with is the fact that there is next to no support for, or understanding of, fibro (in Ireland). You can only be diagnosed by a rheumatologist, for which the waiting lists are months long even if you go privately. Ireland does not recognized fibro as a long term condition. Somebody with fibro cannot claim disability. There are efforts being made by campaigners to get it added to Ireland's LTI (Long-Term Illness) scheme. This would mean that sufferers could receive a medical card or GP visit card. Unfortunately, when the issue was raised in the Dáil (Ireland's Parliament) in May 2016, Health Minister Simon Harris said, "Fibromyalgia is not one of the 16 conditions covered under the long-term illness scheme. There are no plans to extend the list of conditions covered by this LTI scheme," either. In 2018 the position has still not changed.

Every minute of every day I am in pain. It's not always severe but it's always there. It could be throbbing legs or shoulders, a sudden sharp pain in my ankle or hip, stinging or burning eyes, or bursitis. *It never stops.* I honestly don't know what it feels like not to be hurting somewhere.

What is not widely understood either is that painkillers don't work. There is regular nausea, debilitating fatigue, and anxiety. The thing is, I can cope with the pain and nausea and even fatigue, though it can be severe. What I struggle to cope with most is extreme agitation. When I wake up on a beautiful weekend itching everywhere, having an irritated throat that I have to repeatedly clear, having my heart race, my fingers not working properly because I can't grasp anything without dropping it, my words coming out wrong and my sensitivity to sound is at its peak I'm overwhelmed. I feel like I need to screammm... To date, I have found nothing to help me with this, nor anyone to take it seriously. At times like this, I can fully understand why people decide to end it all. When I feel like this, I don't know what to do. I don't want my husband and daughter to have to put up with me. I can't tolerate being near anyone. The slightest noise of Ronan swallowing his coffee or Eliza chewing her cereal makes me so angry that I can't breathe.

It's taking over my life. Sometimes I feel like I don't talk about anything else. It feels like the reason I exist is to facilitate this disease!

How Many More
Will This Ghost Hurt?

By Chemain

As I read the poem you'll have the opportunity to read (after this chapter), it bought me to tears. My first thought was how wonderful that my own daughter can put on paper words that cannot only express what she is thinking, but also the emotion behind them. However, once that amazement passed I then sat and thought about what the words mean to me...the pain I see in her eyes when I am unable to get out of bed, how my husband constantly says, "Don't worry, you will get better" and hates the word "disabled," and how my beloved son would rather not be around me at all as he does not know yet how to process the person in front of him from the one he knew only 18 months ago.

I suppose I should start at the beginning and that definitively started in March 2017. I was in Manchester, England, visiting the University of Manchester to discuss possible faculty and student partnerships, with the Director of the Masters' of Arts Program in my school at Indiana University. We had the most amazing, informative, and eye opening day with the staff and faculty of the university and partners of theirs in Central Manchester. We were both so struck by how inclusive the university was, through their museums, connections and social programming, with the different ethnicities and cultures in and around Manchester. The six miles or more we had walked around Manchester felt like nothing and the amazing food and conversations in the local pubs were inspiring.

That was Wednesday March 6, 2017, and on Thursday March 7, 2017, I could not get out of bed. My whole body was screaming and I felt like I had been hit by a bus. At first, I thought it was the

Polymyalgia Rheumatica I was diagnosed with in September 2016 acting up. But then the questions started filling my mind. Did I need to take more steroids? Can I do that without asking my doctor? I thought the Polymyalgia Rheumatica only affected the upper body. Why did my legs feel like they could not carry me anywhere? How was I going to go to our spring break program in Berlin feeling like I did? And after all of this went through my head I fell back asleep. Why was I so tired? More than tired?

I never made it to Berlin, Germany, for the spring break program due to a number of strikes by airline and terminal workers and, as it turned out, it was a good thing I did not. I eventually headed home on the following Monday and was so pleased to see my daughter at the airport to pick me up, I was a mess physically and emotionally. My own bed felt so good, once I had pulled myself up the circular staircase, and that is where I spent the next few days until my husband came home from a trip to Mexico. Thank goodness my daughter was living with us at the time as she was able to take care of the dogs and me around her work schedule. I was useless! I did have to pick up my husband at the airport and when we got home and I pulled myself out of the car and wobbled toward the door he wondered what was going on. I had told him I was not well, but not exactly all the symptoms.

I returned to work on Wednesday March 13, 2017, and tried to battle through the pain, fatigue and "brain fog" I was experiencing. Needless to say, by the next week I was home and there I stayed for ten weeks while I fought with doctors and my insurance company to get through what seemed like hundreds of tests and to be diagnosed with fibromyalgia. Apparently, I never had Polymyalgia Rheumatica, or so the ER neurologist told me, and then my rheumatologist. As ALS and multiple sclerosis had been discussed I was pleased it was fibro. As shown on the television advertisements I would take Lyrica and my life would return to normal...well, many of you know how that really goes! Lyrica did nothing for me and I was started on Gabapentin and Cymbalta and slowly felt somewhat better.

Back to the damn "fibro fog/brain fog." I was teaching a masters course at the University of Indianapolis one night a week. I completed my masters in adult education with the sole intention of being a facilitator for adult learning. It also helped me move up to Director of the International Office for the School of Public and Environmental Affairs. The sheer embarrassment and frustration of standing in front of a class of adults and not being able to recall essential words and elements of the subject you are teaching. My students saw me leave for my trip in March as a vivacious, highly driven instructor who enjoyed learning with and from the class. I returned a broken, slow and exhausted person who could not even stand to teach. To lose my words as I did then and do now, especially if I am meeting someone new, is probably the most difficult for me to handle. There are always so many projects happening within my team and I can no longer recall information as I used to. I know where to find the answers, but I never had to look anything up before. I am broken…

I returned to work in June 2018, worked two, then three and finally five days a week, but could not keep up with the 40-hour weeks in my office. Very long story short, I started to work from home one day a week, Wednesdays, and managed a maximum of six to seven hours in the office on the other days. I was so lucky that my job allowed me to do this and my team was amazing throughout. However, I know that those days when I needed to be wheel-chaired in from the car after my 40-minute drive home, or the evenings I fell asleep while getting into bed, now downstairs in the old office as stairs don't work for me anymore, days I could not be woken to eat and the days I cried in pain, did hurt those around me. Especially my loved ones.

Fast forward to now and I am still in pain and my employer is now talking FMLA and ADA as I still cannot do a full 40 hours in the office. My darling husband does all the cleaning, cooking, shopping, and caring for our three pups as I live to work. I am so scared I may lose the ability to work, thus my identity, my sense of accomplishment…finally the *ghost* will take what I have left to enjoy. I walk with a stick or a walking cane for short distances and use an electric wheelchair at work so the ghost, per se, remains at a distance. The pain, fatigue, weakness, numbness, tingling, searing pain on my face and ear, and the sense of ants crawling on my legs (ants that are not there) I wish were not apparent to my family. I wish I could hide all my symptoms from them. I try so hard not to yell, as my legs jump around uncomfortably from restless leg syndrome, or my ribs feel as if they are being crushed and I cannot breathe, or due to sheer frustration because I cannot do something I used to do before with no problem. I try not to come home from work and show my depleted, snippy, moody self. I try not to push my pups off me as they hurt when they lay too hard against me or want me to continue to stroke them. My hands cramp up and my frustration at them or the food my husband so amazingly provides each night may not be what I want or is not prepared as I like it. It is when I am not able to hide these things, that I know my family sees the pain, hurt, frustration on my face. I am one that wears her heart on her sleeve, my face tells everything, so I know I am not trying hard enough. My staying off work was because I truly cannot form a sentence on some days, which also makes me depressed. Sometimes the words I use instead of the correct word can be extremely comical and my family laughs along with my embarrassed laugh. I know it brings them pain and I am letting them down.

I do not want my family to worry about me, I am the wife, the mother and soon the grandmother and I should be looking after them! Fibro has taken away my chance to be there for them 24/7. Not being awake when they need me, not being able to go and be there for them, and, what I am so scared and emotional most about, is not being able to hold my first grandchild. It is then that I do hate my body and wish that this disease had not chosen me. It has not only changed my life, but more importantly my family's life. I have not cooked a meal for my husband, or my children, since I returned from England. When not at work, I am either in bed or my recliner. I can no longer do the things I loved to help with around the house, such as helping in the garden, blowing leaves, playing with the dogs or even going for a car ride and looking around one of the plant nurseries with my husband. Drinks do have to be opened for me, my meat needs to be cut up for me, and I cannot even open a bottle of wine for myself.

Selfishly, I miss traveling across the world with my job, I miss not having my hair colored as sitting in the hairdresser's chair for too long hurts. I hate having gained 40 lbs and not being able to wear the clothes and beautiful high heels I used to. It is the pain in my husband, daughter, and son's eyes that hurts the most about this disease. I try to laugh and find the silver lining in everything, but my daughter is right laughing hurts too. So I will continue going to the doctors and rheumatologists and play with medications until, maybe, I feel better and will pray that my daughter is never visited by this *ghost*. It would be more than I could bear…

The Pain That Took Her From Us...

What's wrong, Muma?
"I hurt."
How are you feeling, Muma?
"I hurt."
I try to understand the pain,
The complete agony,
The agony that has taken over,
Over the face that once smiled,
Laughed,
And lived.
The fact that this ghost,
A ghost that NO ONE,
Not anyone can see with their eyes,
Has taken you from us,
From yourself
From what you love.
To live a life that you hate.
Makes me hate your body,
Miss your smile,
And worry constantly.
Worrying selfishly that I may,
May attract the same ghost,
Or it may attack my unborn child.
I worry if you can drink,
That drink may have a lid you cannot open,
Or that you are eating.
Feeding yourself, requires standing.
Standing makes you hurt,

Sitting makes you hurt,
Crying in pain makes you hurt more.
The worst is that I cannot make you laugh,
Because it will hurt you.
"FUCK YOU, FIBROMYALGIA!"

By Danielle Amantecatl

Fibromyalgia,
The Relationships It Stole

By Tamara Everhart Smith

Ask any fibromyalgia patient what this condition has taken from him or her and you are likely to hear some of the same answers over and over. They'll talk about the fatigue, the pain, the strange tingling sensations, their loss of sight, thinning hairline, and gastrointestinal issues. It's well known among the fibro community that we all have trouble sleeping, difficulty with resuming our normal daily activities, and have even had to adjust our occupations, if not quit working altogether. This information is readily available to anyone with the inclination to do the tiniest bit of research.

When your doctor diagnoses you, these are the symptom you'll hear about. Beyond that, however, is a dark underbelly of what fibro does to a person. Fibro has stolen so much from me. It has taken my strength, my confidence, my beauty, my sense of belonging, my future and my goals. Fibro has changed my life in ways I never imagined for myself. I never thought that by the time I reached my thirties, I would be unemployed, halfway through a bachelor's degree, navigating a life through the murky waters of an often "misunderstood illness." Those disappointments and unforeseen obstacles have changed me. The real suffering, however, comes from something else entirely. The part of fibro people don't talk about is the way it changes your personal relationships.

Fibro has always been misunderstood by people in and out of the medical community. People suffering from fibro have often been brushed off, dismissed or worse. Their ailments are said to be psychosomatic, and the patients have been called hypochondriacs. Of course, people with fibro are hurt, angered and discouraged when doctors, employers or acquaintances make these comments. It can be very upsetting and make us question our own sanity or self-worth. I've left a doctor's office feeling like there's no point in ever going back. I just knew the doctor and his staff were sitting around talking about the crazy chick with "fibro," using air quotes to convey their disbelief. I've seen the look on their faces as they hold back and try not to roll their eyes. I've felt the condescension in their voices when they said there is nothing they can do for me. They suggest that I just diet and exercise and that the whole thing will work itself out. They tell you that you'll be okay, and you just need to think positively.

While these situations can be frustrating and painful, at the end of the day those aren't the people we carry with us in the parts of our minds where we hide our insecurities, disappointment, and sadness. We can make an appointment with a different doctor. We can hide our diagnosis from our bosses. We can smile politely, excuse ourselves and walk away and find a different person to make small talk with at the party. Our friends and family aren't as easy to replace or forget.

"You don't look sick."

"We all get tired from time to time."

"You just have to push through it."

"Oh, wow, you're actually out of bed today."

"At least you don't have a serious disease."

"It's all in your head."

"Fibromyalgia isn't even a real disease."

"You need to see a psychiatrist. Once you have your anxiety and depression under control, these things will work themselves out."

"What did you do all day?"

Admittedly, some people may think that their words are helpful. They think they're only being blunt. They may intend for their comments to be motivating. Or, at times, people just speak without thinking and put their proverbial foot in their mouth. Sometimes, these statements do come from a good place. Well-meaning family and friends will say things like, "You just have to get it out of your head that you're sick." Their heart is in the right place, and it may sound like an innocent enough comment. Sometimes, it's even worse. The way our loved ones' cope with this illness changes from family to family, person to person. However, the damaging effect it has on the level of trust can be very difficult to repair. Those of us with fibro spend our days fighting our own bodies. The last thing we want to do is fight our friends and family, the people we love, the people that are supposed to be there for us.

Before I got sick, I lived a full life. I was a college student. I had a part-time job in the family business. I was a wife, a mother, a sister, a daughter, and a friend. I took my children to play dates with other moms. I met the girls for drinks on the weekends, sometimes drank too much, and always laughed and had a good time. I had so many men and women on my side. They were always there for me, and I for them. Then I got sick.

The first few times I went to the emergency room in pain, or with some unexplainable symptom, everyone was concerned. My dad sent me flowers. My mom made me dinner. My best friends called me a few times a day, asking if I was okay. My extended family kept up with me, worried for me, afraid that something might be wrong with me. Everyone had me on their prayer list at church. We all feared but tried not to think about the idea that, something might be wrong. The emergency room visits continued, but nothing was found. The doctors didn't know why I was hurting. They discharged me with different medications to control my symptoms and vague terms thrown in my direction to explain them, none of which were concrete.

Doctors sent me for MRIs, Cat scans, blood work, and other expensive tests. At first, my family was eager to do whatever it took to find out what was wrong. My parents were more than willing to pay for the tests, and any meds prescribed. They were scared for me and wanted to do whatever it took to figure out what was wrong. Then, just like the emergency room visits, the tests produced no results, and we all grew weary of the process. Understandably, my parents were frustrated with spending so much money on my quest for a diagnosis, but their expressions of frustration came out like accusations. I started to feel guilty for the money I needed. I had to take more caution in weighing the seriousness of my symptoms before running off to the emergency room or to see a specialist.

As a young woman with no idea what was wrong with me, it was difficult to discern when a symptom was truly indicative of an emergency. Although my symptoms often went unexplained, this wasn't always the case. Sometimes, the ER staff found a troubling, legitimate condition. Once, I had a life-threatening DVT, also called a blood clot, in my left arm and spent three weeks in the hospital. Another time, I caught a severe case of pneumonia. It was so serious; the hospital had to admit me and treat me with IV antibiotics for two days.

Even with instances of serious, indisputable illness, my friends and family questioned how sick I really was because I had no "real" diagnosis. They thought fibro was a made up disease and used by the medical community to explain nonexistent illnesses. Some of them called me a hypochondriac, implied that I was drug seeking or made passive aggressive digs. I was going through hell, scared, in pain, and watching my life fall apart around me, and I felt like the number of people I could depend on was plummeting rapidly.

I stopped telling them when I was sick. I stopped asking them to babysit my children, so I could go to the emergency room. I stopped asking for financial help with my medical bills. Instead of pushing through, I just dropped out of college, canceled plans, ignored texts, and made excuses for missing birthdays. I had to save all my energy for cooking, cleaning, and tending to my children. I didn't feel motivated to spend my limited strength on people, especially if we had grown apart.

About six months after I first got sick, I had a terrible ear infection. I was off my feet for days, in pain, infected, and miserable. To lift my spirits, a friend invited me to watch a play. I've always loved the theater and seeing a play never failed to improve my mood. I didn't want to go, at first, since I was so sick. My friend encouraged me. "You haven't left the house in days. It will be good for you. You won't be on your feet, so you'll technically still be resting." I debated back and forth, finally deciding to go. My friend was right. I wouldn't be doing anything except sitting in the audience, so it wouldn't take much out of me. It seemed like a good idea, until later. I remember coming home that evening and my husband was upset with me. "You couldn't clean the house, but you could go to a play? I guess you're not really that sick, after all." At first, I was so hurt that he felt that way, but I eventually understood. It made sense for him to resent me for choosing to go out and do fun things, depriving my family of my time and money, when I was contributing so little to my household. He carried the burden of providing for us, financially, and often had to compensate for me when I wasn't well enough to do my part around the house. He never said that he didn't want me going out, but I could read between the lines and see that he needed me to save my strength, time and energy for my family. Things had changed.

At first, my friends tried to accommodate me, and come to visit me at home. Girls' Night changed from dinner and drinks at a restaurant or bar to dinner and drinks on my back porch. They all worked together and threw me a birthday party at home, saving me from having to get out and about. My friends were sweet enough to keep inviting me out, even though I could rarely accept. They tried to check up on me regularly. After a while, "How are you feeling today?" seemed like a silly question to ask, since the answer was always the same. It became more difficult to lift my spirits, and I had less and less to contribute to conversations. I normally turned down invitations, so they stopped asking. My more superficial friendships faded considerably.

The friends that stuck around, however, started to feel more like family. I wouldn't say that I lost any friends due to my illness. The friendships that faded were superficial, so they were likely to be short lived anyway. The friendships I've held onto, now, are of a different dynamic. Now that I've had time to adjust to my new way of life, I'm able to navigate more carefully the tricky dynamics of maintaining friendships as a chronic illness patient.

However, there is something sacred about the friendships that managed to survive the transitional phases of my life between my times of health, the unstable times of diagnosis, and the life I have now where fibro has a permanent home. It's a rare and beautiful thing to find people with whom you share such a special relationship that your fondness for each other can survive unfair reciprocity, extended periods of absences and the need for selflessness. It would take the rest of my life for me to properly convey the appreciation I have for the people who have managed to continue to love me, despite my illness. Not all relationships can withstand such pressure.

If fibro can take a toll on friendships, you can only imagine what kind of damage it can do to a marriage. My first marriage ended about a year after fibro's crude entry into my life. I would be dim to think that fibro was solely responsible for the failure of my marriage. Obviously, a marriage with a firm foundation of love, respect, and maturity can survive a chronic illness. But it would be equally silly to believe that the burden of my illness, shared by both of us, didn't factor into the failure of my marriage. My ex-husband told me, the day he asked me for a divorce, the reasons he cheated on me. "She cooked me breakfast. She tried to take care of me. She ironed my work clothes. She said she doesn't see why you don't do these things, especially because you don't have a job. You don't pull your weight."

He was right, of course. I didn't iron his work clothes. I didn't wake up to make him breakfast. I didn't take care of him. It took everything I had to get out of bed in the morning. Sometimes washing my hair was a chore that took me an hour. I had to put all my strength into caring for the children every day. Other times, it was all I could do not to lie in bed and cry. I couldn't blame him for feeling the way he did. It's more than that, though. I've spoken with many other people who have told me that their romantic relationships were pulled down and damaged because of this illness. Fibro causes anxiety, depression and mood disorders. Naturally, your spouse is the person most likely to feel the effects of that. I was, especially at the beginning of my illness, easily brought to tears, angry with my circumstances and withdrawn. My emotional instability made for a less than perfect wife, to say the least. The husband or wife of a fibro patient often carries the financial burden alone. That stress can be a lot for someone to carry while dealing with the additional stress of medical bills, doctor's visits and an endless list of symptoms from your spouse, especially when you're in your early twenties, with two small children.

·While learning to cope with fibro, I was desperate to continue to be a loving, attentive and intuitive mother. I carried my failures deeply and felt a staggering amount of shame in my inability to be the same mother that I was before I got sick. No matter how difficult it became, though, I did what mothers do. I endured. I can't say for sure that my children agree, but I've done all I can to keep my illness from affecting them too much. My children were young, so they didn't notice too much that I did so much less for them while I was trying to learn to live with my illness. I almost think it's better that I got sick at the beginning of their lives. This version of me is all they know. I can imagine that it would be more difficult for children to adjust to the limitations of their mother having fibro if it hadn't always been that way. I can't say it hasn't caused them problems. The nature of fibro isn't one long, continuous sickness. Sometimes, we are well and then a flare hits us like a ton of bricks and knocks us down. A fibro patient can go six months to a year feeling healthy, then fall ill. My kids, growing up, would forget that I was sick, they must adjust all over again to me getting worse. They realized that I couldn't do what other moms could do. Sometimes, I couldn't play soccer like I did the day before. Other times, I couldn't make homemade desserts the way I had the week before. I sometimes must spend more time in bed, and less time playing. But overall, my relationship with my kids has stayed consistently positive and full of love. There are parts of me, though, that feel regret for the life that could have been.

If I had known it was my last good day, before I got sick, I would have planned out a perfect day of being the mom I've always wanted to be. I would have taken them to the park, and instead of finding a shady spot on a bench, out of the sun like I normally do, I would have climbed on the playground equipment and cherished every squeal of delight as I chased them around. I would have taken the kids for a walk, and not had to worry about resting before and after to compensate for the energy it took. I would have climbed a tree with my son, and I would have had a dance party with my daughter. I would have had a campout in the living room, falling asleep on the floor with the kids. I've still managed to push through and do those things with them since then, but I am unable to enjoy it or do it without modification.

I've had fibro for around six years. In that time, I've learned a lot about how to live my fullest life with this condition. Even with all the research and trial and error, it still has a hold of me in a way that is difficult to explain to anyone that doesn't see it firsthand. Nearly three years ago, I was remarried. My husband knew I had fibro when he met me, but it was in a sort of remission, and I was asymptomatic for the first two years of our relationship. Two months before our wedding, I got my second DVT, ended up in the hospital again and had to quit my job. It was during this hospital stay that I found out that, in addition to fibro, I have lupus. The realization of the auto-immune condition (which has symptoms almost identical to fibro) brought us relief, but it also took us on a whole new journey while we tried to figure out what that meant for our lives, and what our next step would be.

I use the word "our" because the struggles I face in my health are no longer my own, but a shared struggle. Rather than feeling like my illness is a burden I've placed on his shoulders, I view it as a shared struggle. Our marriage has been strong enough to evolve with the climate of my condition, and my husband has evolved, with a strength I didn't know he had. When we met, he was single, childless and virtually free of responsibility. The most crucial decision he typically faced consisted of deciding if he should go out to watch the Rockets play or stay in and watch from home. Now, he is a father, a husband and at times, a caretaker, and he has also become my advocate.

We live a different life than most newlyweds. Instead of weekends away, we do three day hospital stays. We spend many nights on our couch, binge watching tv, so I can be near my heating pad. Oftentimes, date night gets moved from our favorite restaurant to cooking at home and watching a movie. Even though he has accepted these limitations I face with grace, without complaint, I know our marriage isn't completely unscarred. I feel guilty every day for burdening him with the pain, ailments, and disabilities that are my life. I pity him for not having a more capable partner to fairly contribute financially, domestically or in any other way. For the life of me, I'll never understand how he can manage to put up with it. Fibro has managed to taint my relationships so frequently, that I still find myself asking him if he's okay with the life we live. To his credit though, if it bothers him, he hides it flawlessly. We've managed to test the "in sickness and in health" vows of our marriage sooner than most. That truth has made the other parts of our vows to each other feel richer and more meaningful than I had ever imagined.

With permanence much like that of my husband, I can look at a few of the people in my life and see that they've never left. Of course, some people had to come back and try to be a part of my life after I figured out how to live the life of a fibro patient. My sisters and my best friend are almost surreal in their dedication and loyalty to me. They've seen the ugliest parts of me and watched me struggle in ways I would never reveal to anyone else. And they've never questioned me or made me feel like I was less for the troubles I faced. My heart goes out to anyone that's battling this terrible sickness that isn't lucky enough to have what I have in them.

Fibro attacks different parts of my body, organ systems and mind every day. There are parts of me that are changed forever, and parts that I will never get back. My relationships with the people I love, mirror my body in this same way. It is an ever changing, unpredictable course on which we run. The faces of the people standing beside me are much different than the ones from the beginning of this journey. Some are still there, next to me. Some have come and gone. Some are behind me, and some are still up ahead. Fibro, as I previously expressed, has taken so much from my life. I can confidently say though, that the people that are still here have made the other losses I faced worth it in every way. There are physically healthy people that will never know what it's like to be able to look at the people next to them and say that they've already been through a lifetime of "thick and thin" before their lifetimes have even really begun.

A Male View of Fibromyalgia & Pain

By Jack Desoto

"Everybody Hurts"

This is a song that really speaks to me. It talks like a friend who understands how I feel a lot of the time. It's a song that was recorded by R.E.M. I would recommend looking it up if you have fibromyalgia, it just may speak to you as well.

Everybody hurts, but not everyone hurts in the same way. I have a theory that I believe to be true. If we were to switch bodies with someone, we wouldn't be able to tolerate each other's pain because we wouldn't be used to it. Imagine going into the body of someone with chronic pain. I'm not exaggerating when I say that I have days that would probably kill some people. At the very least, this pain would cause these people to wish they were dead.

For me, every day is a day of pain. What varies is the amount. A good day gets a "three" on the pain scale, bad days get a "ten" or more. An average day is a "seven." The good days are few and far between and I always hope that I've turned a corner for the better. The next day, however, I realize I'm not better. Instead, I feel like I've been beaten with a baseball bat. That's my reality with fibromyalgia. Every average day I have to plan out, so that I can make it to the end. I have Ibuprofen and Acetaminophen stashed everywhere: at home, in my office, in my car, in a pill container in my pocket. These pain-killers are the only thing that even touches my pain. The strong stuff like Oxycontin, Vicodin, and Hydrocodone do absolutely nothing for me. I might as well be eating Skittles for all the difference they make. The upside is that there is no danger of me becoming addicted or abusing these narcotics.

For a couple of years, I have been working with my doctor, to figure out how to treat my conditions. I don't feel any better than when we started. If anything, I feel worse, due to the side effects of the medications. Medications that don't seem to treat the symptoms, anyway. As time passes, there seem to be more problems and new issues. Depression is making its presence felt more and just adding to the gloom. I'm exhausted all of the time. I don't know if it's from the medication, pain, fibro, depression, or all of the above. I suspect it's from all of the above.

My History

It would probably be a good idea to give you a little background on my pain and other health issues. This will help give you an insight of my history and experiences. I worked and played hard most of my life. I'm an Eagle Scout and hiked and camped a lot. I played baseball, softball, intramural volleyball, and pick-up football games. I mountain biked and walked everywhere.

I taught preschool for years and ran around with the kids, up and down off the floor, dancing and playing. Later, I worked in a warehouse and mailroom. I regularly lifted over 200 lbs by myself and was in great shape. At the age of 33, shortly after becoming a dad for the first time, I blew out two discs and had to have back surgery. That was the end of working in the warehouse, but I went through physical therapy and felt as strong as ever. I still played sports, but I moved to an office job where I sit most of the day. I kept active, remodeling homes, working in the yard, biking, hiking, and swimming. I was generally just busy all of the time. However, times change.

Wracked in Pain

I have had some type of pain my whole adult life, from headaches to muscle spasms, joint pain, and more. My joints pop and crack, along with freezing up or being tender to the touch. I realized some of the pain was the price I had to pay for pushing myself. Ever since I was in my 20s, I have had "normal" headache migraines. A few years ago I started having ocular migraines. At first I was afraid I was having a stroke, because I would lose vision over the course of 30 minutes. Once we figured out what was happening I could feel them coming on and prepare myself. I did have to pull over while driving once, to sit it out, until I could see clearly again. I was put on Topamax, but again, the side effects were worse than the ailment. The migraines were occasional, whereas the side effects were constant. About the same time, I was put on high blood pressure medication and a CPAP machine, and (knock on wood) I haven't had any in a couple of years. Placebo effect or a causal relationship? At this point, I don't care, I'll take what I can get.

As stated earlier, 15 years ago, I hurt my back while working in the warehouse. I had a laminectomy to repair two bulging discs. Since I was hurt on the job, I was moved to an office position. I recovered, for the most part, and went back to a "normal" life. I would have back spasms occasionally, but it was just something I lived with. I was able to notice when the warning signs would occur when I was overdoing it and I needed to relax and stretch my back before I injured it more, instead of pushing through it, as I did in the past.

I have instances when my skin will hurt, for lack of a better description. This happens almost daily and feels like I'm coming down with a fever. Sometimes Ibuprofen will help, other times I just have to deal with it. When this happens, it hurts to be touched, some materials are painful, and the hair on my head hurts. I know this probably sounds weird if you haven't experienced it.

I've never been a fan of the winter. I've lived in the Midwest almost all of my life and I'm happy staying inside during the winter months. It's not a matter of being uncomfortable, I just cannot take the cold after a certain point. Hot weather isn't the same. I may be hot and sweaty and uncomfortable, but I can tolerate it. When it comes to cold, it hurts and I reach a point where I practically run inside to warm up. I've yet to discover a pair of gloves or mittens that can keep my fingers and hands warm and pain-free. I've since found out that this is a part of Raynaud's Syndrome. I just thought I was a wimp when it came to cold weather.

Weaker and Weaker

I used to be strong. As stated earlier, I worked in a warehouse and played softball and other sports regularly. I hiked and did a lot of yard work and home remodeling. I used to lift 200+ lb loads into the back of pickup trucks by myself. I hauled a king-size mattress up a flight of stairs, and lifted a washer/dryer into the basement when I moved several years ago.

I didn't notice the weakness at first, because I could still "flex" my muscles. I knew I had lost some strength, but I wasn't working for eight-plus hours a day, lifting inventory all day. I found out the hard way when I tried to move another dryer by myself and fell down the stairs with it. Turns out, I have high muscle tone, which makes the muscles hard and look good, but they are pretty worthless when it comes to using them. I feel bad having to have others lift things or carry them into the house for me. I feel as if others judge me when people are moving things or putting things away and I'm sitting to the side. Trust me, I wish I could help, but I just can't do it. I feel as if I need a sign around my neck that says "This person has intense pain and weakness." I look okay, but I'm really limited in what I can do. I feel like people look sideways at me when my wife or daughter load things into the car or do yard work.

New Problems

Fast forward to a couple of years ago, when these new, more severe, problems began. I started having limited mobility in my joints. I can no longer throw a ball overhand and have trouble tying my shoes or reaching my back to wash. My left shoulder is in pain most of the time. Sometimes it feels achy, other times, it feels like a metal rod is being jammed into the joint. My arms and hands sometimes feel like when you plunge into a cooler full of ice to get a drink at the bottom. They cramp and hurt. I have times where my skin hurts, for lack of a better description.

Being touched, clapping my hands, and some clothing is all painful during these times. I have a similar feeling when I have a fever, but I don't register having a temperature during these flare-ups. In the last couple of months, I've begun noticing twitches in muscles, and that has me spooked. In addition, I also have the sensation of icy cold on my skin, as if my scalp, arms, and areas of my back are chilled, even if the rest of me is hot.

I have had MRIs, X-rays, ultrasounds, blood work, and other tests, along with physical therapy and I know no more than I did two years ago. I've been to my doctor, a rheumatologist, and have spoken with a surgeon. The frustration and pain are tearing me down physically, mentally, and emotionally. The fibro fog is a real problem, as I write for a living and not having words at my fingertips or losing my train of thought makes my job even more difficult.

Didn't Ask For Help

I was a single dad when all of these issues started, raising my daughter for ten years by myself. I was used to doing most things myself. My daughter helped as she could, but in the end, she was just a kid and could only do so much. I did the cleaning, cooking, car repairs, parenting, teaching, and everything else that comes with being a single parent. I didn't go to the doctor much (or at all, if I'm going to be 100 percent honest) for a variety of reasons such as cost and time. Plus, I'm a man, and according to society, I should just suck it up. In addition, I just chalked it up to getting older.

Then I met the woman who would become my wife. She's a nurse and encouraged me to go to the doctor. I have been meeting with my doctor for about three years, trying to find out what is going on with me. I've been diagnosed with fibro and have been put on Gabapentin, which had worse side effects than the treatment, so I've begun the process of weaning myself off of that to try something else. We still don't know what is going on with my shoulder and now there are other issues that are related to the pain that are surfacing.

This pain and lack of energy have impacted my daily life at home and work. I've become depressed, which doesn't help with either of these issues. I feel like I'm just swirling towards a bad end. By that, I don't mean self-harm, but that I'm going to end up having to be taken care of. That doesn't sit well with me. I've always been an "I'll do it myself" kind of guy.

Treatment Worse Than the Problem?

I hate taking medication and at this point, I would rather just suffer from the symptoms than deal with the side effects. My brain fog and pain are taking a toll on my family life, work life, and social life. I just want to sleep all the time as the mixture of pain and medication just makes me exhausted. I'm a writer by profession, but I can't focus and it is taking me longer and longer to get tasks done. As for my social life, I avoid a lot of activities because I don't have the energy for it or I am in a bad mood due to the pain. People that don't understand will; shake hands too hard, squeeze your shoulder in a greeting, even hugs are excruciating on some days. I've always been protective of my personal space, but now it's a matter of survival!

I'm a newlywed and this combination of pain and exhaustion is not the honeymoon period I imagined. I'm sure being around me can be unpleasant at times. I try not to be short or crabby, but sometimes the pain overcomes my manners. Being intimate is difficult. It's hard to be in the mood when you hurt or just want to sleep. I know guys are supposed to want sex all the time, and I love my wife very much, but there are some days I just want to curl up in the dark by myself. When we do have time together, I worry about it being satisfying for her, as the pain limits the things we can do and the amount of time I can do it. She says she understands and is patient, but it still bothers me that I'm not the man she deserves sometimes.

Just add it to the list of things I don't do well anymore, or can't do at all. I just want to get back to a normal life where I get things done and have some energy. I'm fine dealing with the pain, I have been doing that for almost 30 years and, although I was in pain, I feel like I was productive. My wife would get irritated with me because I wouldn't sleep in and would work on things until it was time to go to bed. Now, I have trouble getting out of bed and just want to move to the couch to take a nap shortly after I do get up.

I feel like a burden to those around me. I'm not suicidal, but I am depressed and think about how better off those around me would be if I wasn't around. There has to be some solution to all of this, this is not the life I want to live and it's not the life I imagined.

Looking on the Bright Side

There have been a chain of diagnoses that have led to other discoveries. The ocular migraines led to a diagnosis of sleep apnea, thanks to an alert eye doctor. I was given an eye exam when the ocular migraines were occurring and he noticed that the nerves in my eye were starved for oxygen and recommended that I get a sleep study. I now wear a CPAP machine when I go to sleep. Around the same time, I was diagnosed with high blood pressure and high cholesterol. Thanks to a mixture of the CPAP, medication, and healthier eating, those are getting under control. The ocular migraines have stopped, but I still have the occasional headache migraine. Who would've thought that a "normal" migraine would be something to celebrate?

I'm better at giving advice than taking it, so here you go: if you don't feel right or feel like yourself, go tell someone. It may take a while, but you will find someone that understands. Just knowing that I wasn't alone was a relief to the point that I shed tears when they said, "Oh yeah! I feel like that too!" Be good to yourself and good to others, that's all we have control over in this world, I think. Peace.

Why Will They Not Believe Me?

By Naomi Wilkie, *Scotland*

Have you ever been told your fibromyalgia is all in your head? I have and much more... I believe my problems with fibro started from when I was in a car accident. I was approximately 15 or 16 years old. Following the accident, I ended up with bad whiplash and a severe burning pain in my neck that went down my spine. The result, a lifetime of terrible headaches. "The pain I was getting everywhere else was just caused by the accident," or that is what I was told by the doctors. I was also told the pain would go away, but it didn't for months. Sometimes just taking Paracetamol would help, other times it didn't touch the pain and I was in tears. Eventually, the doctor put me on strong painkillers and a rub to be applied to my neck and back. Talking with my friends and family you would think it was the Spanish inquisition they believed I was imagining things and thought my pain was all in my head. This wasn't the first time I had heard this and I'm sure it will not be the last. *Did they think I just wanted time off school?* To be honest, if I wanted off school I only had to tell my mum I wasn't feeling well. Since I had been experiencing pain for a while my family and doctors thought they were just grow-ing pains. Even at school, they thought I was making everything up with a look that said "whatever...we don't believe you." After four or five months I was still getting the neck and back pain. Nobody had an explanation. Instead of getting better other medical issues arose. I don't know if my new issues were related to the same accident, but I was diagnosed with Irritable Bowel Syndrome (IBS). I then started getting crippling spasms in my stomach that again led to the bottom of my spine. This would get worse at certain times of the month. I was put in the hospital quite a lot, the nurse and doctors would look at me like they were thinking she couldn't be in that much pain. (I would sometimes look back at them thinking *"I'd like to see you handle this."*)

The next few years consisted of having three laparoscopies where they found I had endometriosis. I was even told I couldn't have children which explained why I had lost a pregnancy. My body was just being evil to me. My mum had died, my world had caved in and I went "off the rails." My dad couldn't handle me anymore, so he sent me to England to stay with my aunt. My pain started to improve, but after seven months I had to move back to Scotland because my dad had fallen sick.

I still had not been told that I had fibro I don't think they knew what was wrong with me. With all the different medical issues I had and the previous accident I was taking longer to recover after each operation. Eventually, however, I managed to handle my pain and moved back to England to live with my aunt.

I got married in 1995. Not long into my marriage it was suggested I start hormone treatment, the doctors thought it might help reduce the pain I was feeling in my stomach. They told me if hormones did not work my next course of action would have to be a hysterectomy. It turned out I could not even start the treatment because I was pregnant. I thought the nausea I was experiencing was because of all the pain medications I had been taking but it turned out to be a pregnancy. It took several tests and an appointment with the gynecologist to make us believe my body was capable of a pregnancy. It took more tests before doctors believed me. I felt very tired, it was debilitating, but I believed it to be due to the pregnancy. I was in the hospital a few times due to the pain, but doctors said the pain was due to possible miscarriages. During and after my pregnancy there were still different medical symptoms going on that doctors couldn't explain.

My pain was getting worse, and spread to different parts of my body. My joints were starting to hurt also. My doctor just looked at me, nodding his head, like he didn't believe me. My family started to do the same thing. I was referred to a psychologist, I felt they wanted to prove it was all in my head. My health advisor would say. "Oh, you're just feeling run down and tired." My husband, children, and

I moved back up to Scotland when he had lost his job. Having my family around I started to feel less stressed and the pain was reduced. My marriage, however, did not last because my husband could not find a job and found living in Scotland difficult due to my health, the children and the different cultures. I found myself single, a mum of three children very close in age. Not surprising, my stress and pain levels returned.

A few years later I got remarried, but my symptoms returned and they said that the endometriosis was back. Unfortunately, two days before my wedding, I had to go to the ER. I couldn't get hold of my partner, as he was in recovery after falling off a tank at work. His muscles, anterior cruciate ligament, and knee had been injured. I was so lucky I had some good friends and one came with me to the ER. The doctors weren't sure what was going on because the tests were normal and then they told me I was pregnant. *Shock and fear* are what I remember because of all the pain I was experiencing. I had three children to look after (my brother and sister and their families had all moved down to where I used to live in England) and felt really alone as I struggled with my health, looking after my children and caring for my dad, who was recovering from a stroke.

My children and I were supposed to move to the Cotswolds with my second husband because he was in the army. (My dad was to go down and live near my sister and brother in England.) The increase in pain obviously was due to stress. I managed to get through my wedding day and my dear friend looked after the children on Sunday so we could have a day-long honeymoon with some friends. We went for a drive to visit some of the beautiful landmarks and have a picnic but, unfortunately, the day was ruined. Pain consumed my body as I had never felt before. I had a few threatened miscarriages and I knew what that pain felt like but this was different. It was like being stabbed in the back and stomach with an awful burning sensation in my back and stomach. Actually, there was pain all over my body. I couldn't cope and could not control my temper. The more stressed I became, the more pain I was in. I ended up at the hospital again and the doctors had no idea what was causing my pain. Eventually, doctors got the pain under control but I was still so upset because it had ruined our day and I thought my marriage was going to be over before it started. We had only been together for four months, we were in our fifth month when we got married and the blood test continued to show I was pregnant. During an ultrasound I learned I wasn't too far along, and one minute the baby was on the ultrasound screen and the next it wasn't.

Doctors said not to worry but to have my local doctor look into things when I got home. My husband had to go back to camp on that Monday because the army wouldn't extend his leave. My family wasn't nearby, and my dad was still recovering from a stroke, so I was on my own. Although my friend lived in a different town, she and her daughters asked me and my children to stay with them. With continuing pain and exhaustion from not sleeping well I ended up being rushed back to the hospital. This time I lost the baby. I had to have a small operation and hoped to leave the same day but was kept in from Friday to Tuesday. Due to the pain and lack of sleep, we ended up staying at my friends for over a month before returning home.

I've never been good at describing how I feel. I know when something isn't right and when I should start feeling better. I was still feeling a lot of pain and exhaustion due to only a couple of hours of sleep a night, while my son was in the nursery. There were a few golden days when I would get about seven hours of sleep but then felt worse! When I tried explaining this to my family, they would ask if I was imagining it and found it hard to understand. The doctors explained that I was in a vicious circle with the pain causing me to feel down, and not sleeping contributed to why I was feeling worse. I was also on strong painkillers, antidepressants, and sleeping tablets. My partner was medically discharged out of the army and was coming home. This caused me to worry because he was only 18 and he didn't sign up for marrying someone older and medically in bad shape.

Again, I became pregnant and we worried things may repeat themselves. I had to be careful which medication I took and I thought things were going well until I was around five months along. My stomach enlarged and was making my back feel so tight and I continued getting the burning sensation in my back. I was also getting a stabbing, burning sensation in my legs and in my stomach it was like my stomach was pulling my back out of alignment. Concerned we called an ambulance. The pain this time was off the charts when they finally arrived. The children were trying to rub my back and legs, while I was rocking back and forth to try and ease the pain, nothing helped. The ambulance arrived but one of medics was so arrogant he just looked at me and actually said: "I was exaggerating the pain." I snapped at him and said "I would like you to try and handle all this pain." He just stared and I felt wrong for calling them, but I wasn't sure if there was something wrong with my baby or not since the pain was the same as when I lost the last baby. Tears streamed down my face and all the medic did was shake his head at me. My friend came to look after my children so my oldest daughter could come with me in the ambulance to hold my hand. My husband followed in the car. We were worried we would miscarry again like our first pregnancy seven months before. When we got to the hospital the first midwife I saw told me "just calm down it can't be *that* painful. If you can't handle this, how are you going to handle being in labor?" (I was thinking maybe she had a point but the more I stressed out the worse the pain got.) They got me another midwife and the doctor came in, but by then I was having an asthma attack. This midwife and doctor were really nice and started to calm me down. Eventually, I was able to tell them what happened, including how I was treated by the ambulance medic and midwife, which they thought was awful.

After my examination, I had an ultrasound and saw the baby was okay. I was happy to know the baby was doing well, but we still didn't know what was causing the pain in my stomach, the bottom of my back and in my legs. By this time, I thought I would never be out of this pain. The doctor believed I might have sciatica, but that wouldn't cause pain THIS bad. In the end the doctor tried manipulating my back which eased it for a wee bit and he ordered a back brace and crutches from physiotherapy. He gave me strong painkillers, with the caution that I was to only take them when it was really bad! Again, the doctors did not understand the pain I was in. *It was terrible* all the time I had not felt pain like it before, even after having my first three children. It was also different to when I had the pain after I got married and lost my baby. There had been five years between my last pregnancy and this one, so obviously my body had changed. As the doctor told me I was to only take these painkillers when the pain was really bad, he also told me to use Paracetamol "in between," and he made me an appointment to see a physiotherapist the following week. The second midwife said to us, "go home and for me to have a hot bath with Radox." If I can use it, which I didn't know if I could or not, but it was worth a shot, and then to get into a warm bed with a hot water bottle and try to sleep for a while.

When we got home the painkillers were wearing off and were due again a half an hour later. My friend helped with my boys as my husband helped me. The boys had been fed. Now the rest of us needed food. I ate a sandwich, and by then, my husband had my bath waiting. My daughter, who was seven, said her brothers were already in bed. I knew she was worried and I told her to eat what her dad had made and then she could help but had to go to bed right after. You could see she was worried and kept checking on me. While I was pregnant, I was awful to my husband, he could do nothing right and I would go nuts at him, but it was because of the constant pain I was in. Eventually, we had a healthy little girl, my pain eased with my pain medication, and happily the way I reacted and treated my husband went back to normal.

My doctor finally put a referral into the rheumatologist and the appointment came a couple of months after my daughter was born. It felt like he didn't have to do too much to diagnose me. He touched certain parts of my body and each time I felt like I would hit the roof. He then told me I had fibromyalgia and chronic fatigue syndrome. I didn't know what they were, but I went home and we told our families what I had been diagnosed with. Their answer to my news was "that's not a real illness, it's something they tell you when they think it's in your head and just want to name it." Again, I was put down and made to feel awful. It was worse when I wasn't sleeping, having bad days and flare-ups to be told I was just being lazy and making things up. On my better days I could use my cane and move around to help, but I was starting to struggle with my left leg as it would drag behind me at times. This made me extremely tired and I couldn't keep my eyes open then I started to shake and I had to be put to bed. Strangely, that's the only time I would get a decent sleep. These symptoms persisted and I could do nothing to fight them, I was eventually sent to a neurologist. It was then I was told, after more tests, some of which came back normal, that I was experiencing non-epileptic seizures. Again, we told our families and again, they made me feel rejected and unloved.

In 2012, I fell ill and I went to see the doctor. He thought I had shingles, so I put the cream on the doctor prescribed, and took some antibiotics. Two days later the rash turned into boils, similar to what my daughter used to get and we were told to burst them, but the new doctor told us not to with mine.

My stomach was turning purple, black and blue and I was screaming in my sleep. I wanted to stay in my dreams because there was no pain there. My family had thought I burst the boils, but I hadn't, the hot water bottle I used to help to ease the pain must have helped them burst. My skin by now looked infected and my husband called the ambulance. I was rushed with lights flashing to the hospital and they said I was septic. Apparently, the bacteria that you naturally carry on your skin all the time had reacted with the bacteria from the boils and I ended up turning septic. I was lucky they had a doctor visiting from Devon and he recognized that I had necrotizing fasciitis something not commonly diagnosed in Perthshire, Scotland. My husband was told if he had left it and taken the children to school and then called the ambulance, I could have died. I am so grateful to the hospital that diagnosed and operated on me. The weeks that followed were hell. I don't remember much about the first few days because I was put into an induced coma. They were trying to give my body some time to heal. When I came out of the coma, they had me on morphine, but that was not enough to help with the pain when they had to change my dressings. They had to use gas and air on top of all the other pain medication they had me on, but as the dressing change included an acid bath to clean it they had to put me on extra pain medication so I could stand it. I also had to have skin grafts done so again the dressings were agony. My threshold to pain used to be good, but since this, I don't have much of a pain threshold.

My dad, sister and brother-in-law came up to help my husband with the children and my supposedly best friend of 35 years also came under the assumption she would help, but as soon as my family left, she did too. I didn't get to see her when I finally got home. Due to the way people acted around me, and the fear of something else going wrong, I panicked easily. I started shutting myself away in my house because of the exhaustion and the pain. I wasn't really coping with it at all and my family has not been up to visit me once. When we visited them the visits were strained, but I don't know if it was because they thought I caused the fasciitis or because of the way they treated me, which was like I was invisible. (It was obvious we weren't wanted around my family.) They have been back to Scotland a few times and I did meet them twice, but I had to meet them in Edinburgh, which was about an hour and a half from me. The last couple of times they have been on holiday in Scotland, my dad, sister and niece visited family about 30 to 45 minutes from where I lived but I never saw them. They even drove past my house! My friends have stopped inviting me to things because I am either too tired, in too much pain or because I would have a panic attack about leaving the house. They really do not understand all of my health issues. The only time I leave the house is for a doctor or hospital appointment.

I have now changed doctors because I feel the first one didn't believe me. She didn't really believe in fibro. I have been told that some doctors do believe in fibro and some doctors don't. If I went to her with a new problem, she said it was due to my fibro so I changed to a different doctor and he has been really great. For a few months, he had a pharmacist come to the house to try and sort my tablets out. We've done this a few times but he's been away at a number of conferences recently so now he has not been around much. Some of the tablets I came off of, I have ended up back on. For example, I was taking Oxynorm during the day and OxyContin in the morning and at night for the pain, but my body got used to it all and when some new part of my body started acting up he would look into it and get X-rays done rather than saying it was the fibro. He has also tried different things for my sleep and suggested other therapies or med-ications for my other problems. When I have bad flares, however, there is not much he can do and sometimes he's straight with me and says adding more painkillers isn't going to help because I'll just get used to a higher dose. I am on approximately 60 tablets a day for my health issues and pain, but at least I am not taking 80+ a day as I was. I now have caregivers that come in three times a week. I need to see if I can get more help during the week because when I have bad days I am on my own and I can go all day without eating and just stay in my room. I have my aids to help me get around the house and depending on the day I will either need to use my cane, my crutches or walker. Some days I have to use my wheelchair, but I try not to use it too much as I don't want to become dependent on it. I take a large number of medications on a daily basis and I know that I can increase certain ones, such as my morphine if I am having a bad pain day. Because I am diagnosed with more than fibro, I take a number of other medications too. The other drugs are for other things, such as my migraines, plantar fasciitis, Raynaud's syndrome, osteoporosis, asthma, anxiety, depression, etc.

I have had fibro for nearly sixteen years and all the looks I get from my family, friends, and strangers make me extremely anxious. My family and friends know what is wrong with me, but they do not want to admit I am ill. There are those who look at me as if they can't tell what's the matter with me and I am panicking, but trying not to let people see it because you don't know what they are thinking. There are other times you are in so much pain you burst into tears or you start forgetting things or mixing things up. I have also put a lot of weight on because of all the tablets, but people don't know that and so they stare. Worse still my children getting bullied at school because their mum is fat and disabled.

Interestingly, there are four of us who grew up hanging out with each other with different stages of fibro. One of them has had it about 16 years also. My other friend was diagnosed about eight years ago and the other one was diagnosed just over a year ago. "*Is it just a coincidence that four people who hung out together in certain places have all been diagnosed with fibro or not?*" We don't know. My sister said to her doctor she thought she had fibro, but then told people she was diagnosed with it but she has not been to a rheumatologist. I thought a rheumatologist was the one who diagnosed people with fibro. My family believes her though and call her all the time to check up on her. I have been treated like crap for 16 years and don't understand why it is different for her and me.

Fibro for me is widespread chronic pain. It hurts my muscles and my ligaments, it has affected my memory and my wellbeing. Simply put, it's pure hell at times and you don't know what to do to feel better. It has affected my family and friends, some that don't seem to care about me and others who don't even bother keeping in contact with me. I lost years raising my youngest two children due to being so tired and in so much pain. They are even fed up with hearing how much pain I am in or how tired I am. I don't blame them because I'm tired of it too. I stay in my room as I don't want to aggravate the pain or worry about hitting into things because my balance is off. Recently, I have been pushing myself a bit more and have started going out a couple of times to shop, or on organized nights at the rugby club, my husband plays for. They don't look at me strangely and don't whisper behind my back, they take me for me, as has my husband's work. Between these two places, I am slowly coming out of isolating myself. I am still getting panic attacks, but once I have spoken to my husband I usually calm down and then I'm okay.

I thought I was finished with getting told it is all in my head, but recently my oldest son started on about my fibro. He had already drunk a half a bottle of wine and I don't know how many drinks he had when he was out eating. He talked about fibro being psychological and that nobody can see our pain and how it would be easy for us to say we are in pain even if it's just a little. He went on to say it's all in my head and he said that I never think about what the children are going through. That is a lie, so I lost my temper with him and he's not been home for the last four years. He has no idea that all I do is think about what having fibro and all the other problems are doing to my children and my husband. (Who on the whole are great when I am told something else has gone wrong, e.g., I am told I now have "tennis elbow.") They do get fed up because it's like nothing gets done about it after I am told, but the doctor has said I need to go to physiotherapy since I *already* go for physiotherapy we have some new things to work on. I do think about my family, what they go through everyday because of my fibro, and how lucky I am to have my children and husband stand by me.

Fibromyalgia is hell. Everyone that has it, goes through their own hell. I just really want to know, "Why don't they believe us?"

The Joys of Chronic Pain

It hurts when I laugh
It hurts when I sneeze
The pain is never at ease.
It hurts when I move
It hurts when I cough
Always, always tough.
It has its ups
It has its downs
Always going round and round
Just like being on a roller coaster.
It can't be seen, only felt
That's what life has dealt.
It wears and tears
And makes you swear.
It makes us stronger
As we deal with it longer
Oh, the joys of chronic pain.

By Lesley King

My Not-So-Invisible Illness

By Clara Aimola Keatings, *Canada*

My name is Clara and I am a 51 year-old woman and I have fibromyalgia. I believe that I have had fibro since I was a child. To begin this chapter, I need to give you a history of my health and medical complications because this is what has led to the onset of my full blown fibro.

I had terrible pains growing up and was constantly told by my family and doctor that it was growing pains. The problem is that the growing pains have never stopped. As a youth and young adult, I didn't let it stop me from living life. I played every school sport that I could, I worked part-time, and I played recreational soccer until I was 39 years old. I landed a full time job, got married to my husband (who is one of the most hardworking people that I know) and had two beautiful, smart children. Myson, who is an artist, and can melt your heart with his eyes and my daughter who is smart and sings like an angel. Both were born by C-sections. I was hurt during my last soccer game (damaged my knee) and that ended my playing sports ever again.

I do have to add that, unfortunately, I've cut people out of my life as they were no longer healthy relationships. Although the pain of having to do this is still very fresh it has improved as time goes by. They say that absence makes the heart grow fonder but, as I have learned, not in all cases. The longer you go without speaking or seeing someone the less you miss or think about them.

I cannot list all of the tests and specialists I went through before I received my fibro diagnosis. (The list would take up my entire chapter.) I was finally diagnosed by my family doctor, a rheumatoid arthritis specialist and by my pain clinic doctor who runs a fibro pain clinic. My brother and uncle have RA and my cousin has fibro so I was not completely ignorant of these diseases, however, I had never fully researched either before being diagnosed.

My cousin with fibro was one of the first people that I called when I was diagnosed, as I knew she would completely understand everything I was going through with my fibro dx. She offered me advice and empathized with me. She understood the pain I was in. I am truly blessed to have her continued support. When the weather is cold or extremely hot my phone rings and it's my cousin simply saying, "Hi sweetie, how much pain are you in today as she is suffering just as much as I am." I hate that she has this disease, but I am also blessed to have someone in my life who knows exactly what I am feeling.

I am very worried about my daughter because she, unfortunately, has started to show symptoms of fibro. She complains about the pain in her hand, neck, feet, and knees. Her menstrual cycle, which used to be light and pain free, is now heavy and very painful.

We need to find a cure! There are many medical professionals who still believe that fibro is not a "real illness" and that the pain we suffer "is all in our heads." There are also some medical professionals who do know fibro is an illness and *bless them* for their dedication and research to help find a cure. These special medical professionals relentlessly advocate for us. There are also many celebrities who also suffer from fibro and they're starting to speak out about what they go through. Lady Gaga has a documentary regarding her pain. The reason I mention celebrities is that they speak out about it via social media and because they have hundreds and thousands of followers, they are actually advocating for us while educating their followers.

I hope and pray this book will help the newly diagnosed by telling them that "this is not all in their heads" and that their symptoms are *real*. They can compare all of their symptoms, feelings, anxieties, and depression with all of the contributors that have written chapters for this book. I also pray that this book will educate family, friends and the medical community. So many families have been torn apart because the family and friends do not understand how fibro affects their loved one. I hope this book will save the families of *all* fibro warriors. We will never give up on a cure!

Here are some things I do that help me deal with fibro: If I am having a good day, I will do some light cleaning or gardening. The trick is to pace yourself no matter what task you are doing. If you clean for a half hour, sit down to take a break for 30 minutes or however long you need. Then go back to your task and repeat the pacing. You will be amazed at what you can get accomplished and will not be completely spent by the end of the day. Have a family meeting and divide up the chores. Decide who takes care of the simple things like garbage, laundry, grocery shopping, etc. Talk to someone when you are feeling depressed or you have anxiety. Don't be ashamed to ask for help, or if your house is not tidy or your laundry is not done. Take short walks, pray, meditate.

When I was referred to the fibro clinic, I was told that the wait was six to eight months. Again, I felt defeated! One day, my son and I were running some errands and at the end, I was in so much pain I could barely walk. The fibro clinic was steps away from where we were. My wonderful son took my hand and said, "Come on, Mom, I am taking you to the clinic." When we arrived, the receptionist said hello and I started crying. My son simply said to her, "Please help my mom." She asked us to have a seat and said she would be right back. She had gone to speak to the doctor. She told me I was placed on the canceling list. God bless my son! Within two days I received a call and I had an appointment within four weeks. That day my son was my advocate and I will forever be grateful for what he did for me.

My experiences include being criticized by a psychiatrist, who made me feel ashamed of my illness. I was already feeling anxious about this appointment and I had already seen one in the past (an appointment for my benefits). I completed the usual questionnaire and the specialist walked into the office and didn't make any eye contact with me. My first red flag. He looked over my questionnaire very quickly and then said, "How may I help you today." I thought to myself that my family doctor must have a reason for referred me to him. So giving this specialist the benefit of the doubt, I explained that I have anxiety and depression and I told him that I have fibro as well as osteoarthritis. He then asked me if I had brought my medications. I took out my bag of meds and gave them to him. The moment he saw what medications I was taking he stood up very abruptly and said, "I am sorry but I cannot help you" and then he left the room. After I picked my jaw off the ground, I started crying. I felt defeated and ashamed and to be honest I was mortified. I got up and left the room. As I was leaving a kind social worker stopped me and asked me if I was okay. I completely broke down. She pulled me into her office and asked me what happened that had me so upset. I explained to her what my visit with the psychiatrist was like. She took my hand and told me that her best friend has fibro and that it is 'not' all in my head. We ended up talking for over two hours! She asked me to try a different psychiatrist and that is exactly what I did. I was very fortunate that our paths crossed at the right moment. I never want to feel that lack of empathy from a medical professional again.

I have been confronted over and over again for parking in disabled parking spots, being both yelled at and humiliated. My children who have not only witnessed these instances but have come to my rescue in my defense. This should *NEVER* happen. I have thought about getting the fibro license plate cover and then thought why should I have to advertise what is wrong with me to the whole world? This truly is an invisible disease and just because I may not look sick doesn't mean that I am not. As if grocery shopping isn't painful enough. The humiliating glares I get when I pick up my meds from the pharmacist on duty who does not know me or my history hurts.

I was asked to have several sessions with an occupational therapist. The therapist was to help me get back to being "normal" and help me go back to work. The therapist was told my medical history as well as all of my other issues I was dealing with including my son. On the third therapy visit, I was advised that we needed to meet outside of the home which can be difficult for me if I am having a bad day. We met at the library on that day. I had brought my son, to give his perspective on what it is like to have a mother who suffers from fibro, and a co-worker/union person, who was there to observe. We were not alone in the room in which we were discussing my symptoms, medical information, and other issues in my life. I was asked what task is difficult for me and I said that grocery shopping is very hard for me. I was then asked what would motivate me to grocery shop. I couldn't believe that someone would think that I am not motivated enough to grocery shop. Believe me I am motivated to do many tasks; however, my illness stops me from doing them. The therapist then pointed to my son and asked me, "What if someone was holding a gun to your son's head and was threatening to kill him, would that motivate you to go grocery shopping." The therapist knew what had recently happened to my son's friend. I could not believe that she had just used that analogy, in front of my son! I started crying and my son was asked to leave the room by my co-worker/union. When she finished talking to the occupational therapist my son was asked back into the room. The therapist apologized to my son and me. (The point I am making is that it is my belief the therapist did not fully understand fibro.)

I try to stay as positive as this disease will let me. Sometimes when I am speaking I realize that, *OMG, what I said may not have made any sense?* Totally forgetting the point I was trying to make. Sometimes when I speak only partial words come out and the rest stays in my mind. This makes me not want to socialize and I've been a social butterfly my *whole* life! I used to have filters but I don't anymore. I have lost many friends because either it takes me days to respond to texts and messages or I may not reply at all, because I do not have the strength mentally or physically to have any type of long conversation. My wonderful family simply pretends to understand what I am trying to say and goes along, although I have been asked, at times, what the heck I was trying to say. Imagine trying to do a job that you don't remember how to do! Or trying to write a chapter for a book but you keep losing your train of thought and your thoughts are all scrambled and all over the place. I still have to live and be a good mother and wife, daughter and aunt, etc. My true family and friends get that if I have to cancel plans or if I do not respond right away it's because I am having a bad day or week.

I started seeing a psychologist who not only talked to me and listened to me but also gave me some tools to help me deal with this disease and all of the symptoms that come with it. Hurray!

It took me a very long time, but I have finally realized that I have to live my life day to day and take the good days with the bad and learn to release the guilt that I feel. I have learned to not worry that my house isn't perfectly clean or that my laundry is not always caught up. I have learned how to rest when I have to and to not overdo it on my good days. I have learned that I can no longer do what I physically and mentally used to and I have tried to accept it. I never totally gave up on myself and I learned how to advocate for myself and to push the doctors for answers and demand specialists listen and get put on cancelation lists, etc.

Thank you to everyone that supports me, prays for me, and with me. There are two quotes that I say *EVERY* morning to myself to help me get through the day.

Out to all of the negative thoughts that I think about.
No one or any place has any power over me,
I am the only one to put thoughts into my mind.
I create my own reality and everyone in it.
I release all things that have caused me any negativity.
I welcome new changes, lessons, and new adventures.
I welcome any new opportunities to grow,
emotionally, mentally and spiritually.

I hope that my words do not make me look weak because I am not. I am a fibro warrior! We are all fibro warriors and we cannot give up hope that one day there will be a cure for our living hell called Fibromyalgia. Do not feel sorry for us but please do empathize with us.

Misguided

By Barb Bickford

Often, your childhood "predicts" your health later in life. My childhood was uncommonly *great*. I grew up in a "father knows best" family. My mom and dad formed a united front on all issues, including the sticky ones. We moved a lot, due to my dad taking different banking jobs, but we always felt we were 'home' because our family of five worked like a unit.

I have a younger brother and an identical twin (bonus)! We were each other's support, guidance, love, role-modeling, friends, and world. I now understand how rare this is. My parents didn't role model "partying, drugs, going out to spend money they did not have." They actually liked all of us having game nights and when my parents did want to be with friends, they had them come to our house or would take us with them (most of the time) as this was still family time.

When I was raped at 17, during my senior year in high school, I was shocked that evil really existed! This shock took me years to overcome and manifested itself with my first marriage. I looked for a person that was good to all his friends and thought that person would be a good companion for life. I truly believed he would never mistreat me. I could not have been more wrong. Control, emotional, psychological, verbal and once physical abuse were reserved for a wife, as I became the target of all negative emotions. (I did not realize, at the time, that my ex-husband saw this behavior in his parents and thought it was a normal way to live.)

At 30, I had my first son. I also had a job at the university that was in my chosen field (BFA with graphic design emphasis and illustration) that I *loved!* My husband refused to let me stay home, even part-time with our son, insisting we get a nanny. I resigned myself to the fact that this was my life. I had already started going to counsel-ing to help our marriage and continued for some time. What didn't continue was the marriage. One night I came running into my son's room because of his screaming and crying. He didn't like baths, and his father was tired of trying to get him to cooperate and was spank-ing him with full strength. (I filed for divorce after that incident and believed that my son and I would continue to live in that town, with me working at my job.)

Counseling helped me to gain my self-esteem back and I focused on my new life and paying the bills.

Eventually, I did remarry and had a second son. I was diabetic while pregnant but the test did not pick that up, so I was never treated. The day my second son was born I developed fibromyalgia and multiple sclerosis. My predisposition from the rape, stress, and abuse from my first marriage and the trauma of being diabetic when pregnant was too much for my body and resulted in these two dev-astating illnesses.

While MS has had reliable treatment for 19 years, fibro was treated by symptoms, and not consistently. This "strange" approach to keeping my fibro "at bay," gave me little help for the pain, sleepless nights, depression at times and exhaustion. We moved several times since my second son's birth. It has always amazed me how little doc-tors knew of fibro.

In the 19 years of looking for help, I have stumbled upon three exceptional doctors. All in different disciplines, one luckily was a rheumatologist. She was a Godsend the ten years I saw her! During that time, I knew I was supported and had a caring doctor.

Once she retired, however, I was thrown in with the rest of the medical community, 85+ percent of whom *do not care* to help an illness that can't be visibly diagnosed and therefore has no defined treatment plan. Instead of being treated as an educated, intelligent person who needed guidance and help, I have had doctors tell me "all I need is a good shrink." Another horrible opinion doctors have stated include "there is no such thing as fibro," and I have actually been turned away from notable medical colleges and their pain clinics or rheumatologists because "fibro doesn't exist" (in their opinion). They flat out won't see me.

In the 19 years I've had fibro, the majority of the medical community have chosen *not* to research fibro to validate its existence, or spend time figuring out how to treat its various symptoms faced by its victims. Really? How sad? Our doctors who took an oath to *do no harm* are indeed harming all fibro patients greatly. By not showing concern for each of us, we are denied help. All because fibro seems too complicated to diagnose and treat. It's easier to not even accept us as a patient than help us. *This does us harm!* In each patient, the harm manifests itself in different ways.

Due to my fibro, I was not able to play with my second son as I could with my first. I had such pain, I couldn't keep up with his activities and had to learn to let him go to childcare to play/socialize with other children and save my energy for a "part" of his day. This truly made me cry!

Halloween, for example, I could make his costume over time, walk a couple blocks enjoying my children's trick-or-treating. Then my husband and my older son would have to take over. Slowly, giving up more each year because of my physical decline. Raking leaves became 'too much' when my youngest was seven or eight, so my older son (by seven years) would finish and I had to watch them enjoy jumping in the leaves through the window, from inside, where I was resting. All these compromises because we fibro patients are "too time-consuming," "too much trouble." I've learned doctors find it's easier to refuse to help us rather than take too much time with one patient.

Do you know who rips apart families? It's not the Republicans or the Democrats, the Liberals or Independents. I know it is not the various religions or people of different cultural identities. It is the established *medical community* that we have been taught are looking out for "our best interests." Instead, however, many flatly refuse to.

The child that isn't treated for his ADD because some doctor, somewhere, years ago, told his dad that *he* didn't need ADD meds. So it filters down to that father, passing ADD on to his son, believing he is right not to allow his son to have these same meds. Even when being medicated showed to help his son do better in school. This father had learned from a misguided doctor years' earlier who did not deserve to be trusted.

It is the doctor who shakes his head at our illness and allows it to progress to the point of a mother needing a wheelchair to get around the college campuses with her second son because she has not been treated as effectively as she could have been. It's the doctors that say fibro is not really legitimate.

Many of us believe our government is guilty of lies and misguided use of our money and time. When in reality, it's the majority of the medical profession that has been deceiving us. They earned their degree, became educated enough to be considered an expert in their field, and we take them at their word, due to their credentials. I contend they are the ones guilty of misdiagnosis, endorsements of toxic pharmaceuticals, and lack of healthy options, as well as increasing rates of disability, declining insurance coverage, and general lower standards of living.

Percentage-wise, the few medical professionals that are *doing good* for us fibro sufferers are "overshadowed" by doctors who are in their jobs "for themselves." I believe the latter are the root cause of a lower standard of living. Think about this: these "pretend to care doctors" affect *every aspect of our lives and society.* Our trust has been misdirected. It is not the politicians we need to worry about. It is the medical providers and the pharmaceutical companies who do not do their best to care for us. Rather, they profit from our illnesses and the medications they prescribe keeping us in a constant state of misery!

Fibromyalgia Looks Like This

By Fiona Young

Fiona Young is an educator, musician, and writer/journalist. She has published a novel and short stories in addition to writing both features and weekly newspaper columns. Her screenplays have received recognition in a prestigious competition. Of written chapter (appearing later in the book) she says, "There isn't much to laugh about with fibromyalgia, but if you don't laugh you'll cry too much. Humor has always been my shield. It's unavoidable when you're raised by British parents!"

Fiona Young has been a photographer for over ten years. Primarily self-taught, her fine art photography has won awards in international competitions and been published in newspapers and professional publications. She also does portrait and headshot work. Her graphics all begin with an original photograph, as in the included images. "The pain of fibro can be difficult to describe," she said. "It's unique to the individual, to the part of the body and differs from day to day. These images are a visual translation."

A New Reality

Fiona Young ©

Fibromyalgia is so complicated no doctor wants to take the time to address every issue and look at a patient as an individual. That is "*if*" you can find a doctor that believes fibro even exists.

Looking at this staircase, you can see how fibro must look to others. The details that surround our illness are overwhelming. It truly is an unending circular event.

Dealing with one symptom at a time would be the ideal way doctor and patient alike can approach treating this illness. By decluttering our symptoms, community understanding and medical empathy for our illness will progress.

Trigger Points

Fiona Young ©

Does this image convey how the medical community makes a Fibromyalgia patient feel? Yes. As a fibro patient, myself, I have been treated with disrespect and disdain.

The doctors have all the power in a doctor/patient relationship and we look to them for guidance. With their power they influence the medical community and effect how us fibro patients are treated. Their disbelief of the very existence of our illness, personally, makes me "feel" like my symptoms are all in my head. Eventually, if believed long enough, we describe ourselves as broken.

A Longer Season

Fiona Young ©

This is an image that I find so important. In this visual, I see myself. I am not the person I use to be, Fibromyalgia has trapped me in a body that does not fit my age. Just as the flowers have a short life, my true self has been allowed to prematurely die.

Where are the doctors who took an oath to do no harm? Each time a doctor dismisses my illness as imaginary, I die a little more. Isn't it time to change that mindset, acknowledge fibro as the disease it is, and allow us to live a healthier life?

Not Your Best Shot

Fiona Young ©

Have you ever experienced a great doctor, when it comes to treating your Fibromyalgia? The word that comes to mind regarding this question is *RARE!*

The windshield in this photo reflects a more familiar reality for fibro sufferers.

Doctors, family, and/or friends tend to react by taking 'shots' at your illness through unkind words, or actions. These "shots" literally make you feel like you would be better off in a junk yard, forgotten. Why? Because the cheap shots that make you hurt, emotionally today, will be the cause of your spirit crumbling and breaking tomorrow.

Shaken Up: Distorted Reality

Fiona Young ©

This bridge conjures up a common image. Nothing out of the ordinary.

Now imagine how the world, not just this bridge, would make you feel if it truly were distorted like the photo. Many patients with Fibromyalgia and other "invisible" illnesses don't show any outward signs of their illness. To the rest of the world, there is nothing wrong.

When you take the time to look through their eyes, however, your world becomes unsafe in a second.

The New Me: Staying Safe

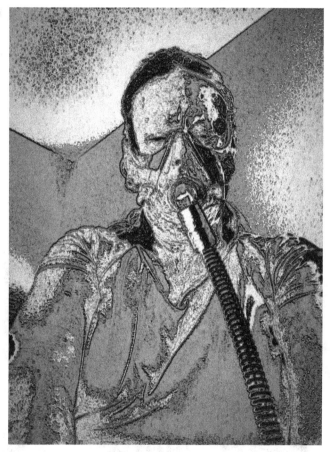

Fiona Young ©

What if your world consisted of having to take precautions, like putting on a gas mask, just to stay living where you do? Would you still want to live there?

It's common for Fibromyalgia patients to take precautions just to function in a world you take for granted. These precautions may be handicap signs, canes, even wheelchairs, or handrails in showers, etc. All are not visible to you, but help us maintain a lifestyle "as close to normal" as possible.

We endure these obstacles, trying not to bring attention to ourselves. Like the gas mask, however, some are too obvious to miss. Unfortunately, even when we don't try to bring the subject of health up, others jump in and make us feel worse with statements like "why do you have a handicap flag on your rearview mirror, you look fine to me" or "save the spot for a disabled person that really needs it." These statements hurt. Greater awareness of and education about fibro will help reduce encounters like this.

Knife, Fork, and Pain

Fiona Young ©

A note about Fibromyalgia: it changes almost everything, including everyday activities like eating. Even something as ordinary as silverware can become a problem.

These shiny objects can cause eyesight problems. Some patients need safer, easier to use utensils. Ordinary silverware can be painful to use, or even completely useless. When you are experiencing pain throughout your body, often hard metal objects can become too much to bear. This problem is simple and easy to fix. Let's fix it so non-sufferers have awareness and understanding of what a fibro patient experiences. Body pain, sight problems, and clumsiness all are symptoms that many fibro sufferers have.

Fibro Felix

Fiona Young ©

That face! This image reflects those emotions that rankle a Fibromyalgia patient's soul: anger, frustration, fear, pain, sadness. Got more? Toss them at Felix! Then go hug your cat, dog, or goldfish.

Pets are the source of comfort and love for many fibro sufferers. They do not look through the eyes of discrimination at an illness they can't see. Instead, they understand and accept you with unfiltered, protective, loyal love. Something the human population could learn from!

Illness and Grief:
The Hardest Relationship Advice

By T. H. Tracy

One of the hardest things about living with chronic illness is learning to live without the life that others take for granted. From the time we are young children, we are conditioned by society to expect our lives to follow a certain path. We will grow up, fall in love, find a career and have a family. While the steps do not necessarily happen in the same order for everyone, everyone does expect these minimal, reasonable chances at happiness. We even plan for them from a young age or fantasize about them. I am not talking about fantasies children have about marrying the prince or becoming a pro-ball player. We imagine our lives as independent adults. We never imagine illness. The dream of being independent and self-sufficient becomes the foundation of adulthood.

My many symptoms began around the onset of puberty; therefore, I never really experienced this self-sufficiency. I have always needed to depend on someone or something. Sometimes I feel like I went from a child to an elderly woman. I skipped that period of life when we are carefree and robust and can depend on our bodies. During that period of my life—from the teenage years to my mid-thirties—I faced frustrating cycles of tests and searches for diagnoses. I would get better and then get much worse. Stubbornly, I pushed forward toward what I envisioned as "normal," going to college and attempting long-term relationships. It was never ending. Like the stages of grief, we have to accept our illness and disability and come to terms with it. We have to find the type of life we can reasonably expect to live and also accept enough to feel whole.

I decided not to marry when I was in my early thirties at the end of a few long-term relationships that had failed. These relationships were unsuccessful because they did not go anywhere, not because they were intense or abusive. They couldn't get anywhere because I could not be an equal participant. I could not contribute half of the relationship, because I was not a whole person. When I was with someone, I would often want to be anywhere else. I would be tired, or my head would hurt, or one of the myriads of symptoms that plague me daily would be flaring up. Oftentimes, talking on the phone would be too hard for me. As supportive as these partners were, I felt like a burden. Sometimes, in attempting to be supportive—but lacking true understanding—the things he said would make me feel worse. "You know, a lot of times when I am sick and I lie in bed all day, I just feel weaker." Hearing "But can't you just talk for a little while?" "I miss you so much!" or "Are you sure you don't want to try it, just for a few hours?" "If you don't feel like driving, I can pick you up!" There was nothing inherently bad in these messages, either in tone or in purpose, yet they made me feel like a failure. Actually, in many ways, he was right. I did need to get up. I just couldn't. I was often very, very ill. The needling was not helping, and the attempts to be supportive had the opposite effect. The pressure of needing to be there for someone else was too much for me. He became anxious about me, and that added to my difficulties. I felt like I was feeding someone else's drama when I could barely cope with my own. How could the two of us make a partnership successful when I could barely make it to a movie? Yet there was something *so* tempting about marriage. He could take care of me. We would share living expenses and household responsibilities, two stresses that caused me major challenges and did not help my health. Living with a person day to day could not be as stressful as having to carve out time, right? We would be there for each other! We would work it out, through thick and thin.

In many ways this was a tempting fantasy, when you overlooked the reality of my illness and his inability to cope with it. I decided it was ridiculous. When he asked me, with tears in his eyes, if I love him? I was not sure how to answer. I was in so much pain and taking so many medications that I was not sure my head was clear. The one thing that I did know was that I could not make a decision like that. The thought of sharing my life with another person did not seem like a fairy tale or even a financial windfall. The one decision I could make was that I was not going to force my life on another person.

I had to put up with the endless doctor visits, hospitals, mystery symptoms, and strange diagnoses. It was my life. Why saddle some other poor soul with that? Out of fairness to him, for the love that I knew I did have for him, I let him go. I was in my mid-thirties and I decided that I had to live the life of a sick person. I would not try to get married. I would not pursue financial independence and career success. I would not try to cure myself. I guess in the stages of grief, I had come to acceptance. I mourned for that relationship, and the others (the ones I never had). I also mourned for the person I never was. I mourned for the person I thought I would be when I was a little girl before I become sick.

This is the reality that many people forget about chronic illness. Chronic illness does not just include pain, in a physical sense, but encompasses emotional loneliness and/or stress, and psychological stress as well. We each have to find a way to accept who we are and find a way to live a life that brings us joy, despite our suffering. Suffering is going to be part of our existence. We will not always have what others have and that is okay. We can carve out a life that makes sense to us and makes us happy, as long as we let go of our expectations of what we thought life "should be" like.

Losing My Professional Identity

By Nicole, *Western Australia*

For me, pain started in my 20's. Physical, emotional, psychological, and medical. I pushed through, never understanding why my health wasn't great. I was happy working, so I ignored that I was truly suffering also.

In 2013, I was headed into a downward spiral which surprised me. I was working in Child Protection but felt like I was on a deserted tropical island. If something went wrong at work, which seemed to happen weekly, I was interrogated by my superior. "What are you doing about your quarterly reviews?," "You haven't written your care plans yet!," "Where are your case notes?" On and on it went.

Meanwhile, my home life was stressed. My husband and I were coming to terms with our son's diagnosis of Autism. While trying to wrap our heads around this diagnosis, we learned he was experiencing bullying at school.

I believe the traumatic, conflicting situations between a career that I loved, my family, and my son's situation at school is when I developed Fibromyalgia. I had symptoms that I had never felt before, "foggy brain," "exhaustion," and "depression." These symptoms felt like they were slowly seeping into me, first in my professional life and then at home.

One day after returning to work from a holiday vacation, I was ambushed by my direct supervisor, my team leader. This particular team leader I did not respect. Actually, of all the team leaders I had worked under, there was only one, over the years, that I did respect. They were all people who worked in Child Protection but seemed to lack the necessary skills needed to lead myself and others. They were all social workers but had advanced to a position without sufficient training. This lack of education caused me and others under their supervision harm. We were not given the guidance we desperately needed.

I left the department in a terribly distraught manner. I decided to look for support and made an appointment to see a psychologist. It was then that I was diagnosed with PTSD (post-traumatic stress disorder). I believe this developed due to the transfer of vicarious trauma. During this same time, I had experienced death threats and a child under my care had been sexually abused. (Looking back at this I am certain that the caregiver had groomed me, so that I had missed certain red flags.)

My life continued to fall apart. I didn't work for about two years. The first year I was away from the department it was considered "leave without pay." I tried to prolong that situation for another year, but was denied. The department wanted a medical report to allow for this "leave status." I was advised by my psychologist not to fight human resources at work. I resigned from my position a short time after that.

Once resigned from Child Protective Services, I worked a couple of short term contracts. I was competent at work, but tired quickly, and soon the pain became more and more of a problem. It was winter and the extreme weather was causing me a lot of pain. Money concerns surfaced as we weren't making the same pay as before. The pay I did make was insufficient. These reduced finances were frustrating and it changed our lives permanently. Guilt, for putting my family in this financial strain resulted in a fibromyalgia flare.

My thinking became negative and always got the better of me. I would wonder, *Could my life have turned out differently?* Thoughts centered around my family and children, then my caseloads from my jobs. I reflected about conversations I had over the years and wondered if I had caused all my problems. *Did I cause this pain? Was it karma?* Self-loathing started seeping into every part of my body. This is what my fibro became. It made sense to me. If I hated myself, then why wouldn't I be in pain?

With all this self-loathing, by 2016 my mental and physical health was deteriorating. I was voluntarily admitted into a private psychiatric hospital. My psychiatrist was great. The hospital experience was not. It was very disempowering and once again my fibro flared. I got the flu on top of everything and that, with the pain I was already experiencing, was too much. I felt that no one was listening and decided to make a statement. Since my doctors were not attentive to me, I threatened the staff by not eating and I put more insulin into my body than I should have. I am a Type-1 diabetic. It was reckless. Due to this physical threat I made, I was seen by a general practitioner. This resulted in the staff managing me as a suicide risk. I saw a GP two days after my request. He did nothing about my flu symptoms. The medication prescribed did work well for my mood but didn't agree with my body. I finally convinced my psychiatrist to discharge me. My husband picked me up and took me home. Over the next two weeks, I reduced my medication to none, coming off them completely.

So here I am again, my severe depressive disorder and global anxiety disorder impacting me. My sense of doom overwhelmed me at an unprecedented level. I started taking my old antidepressants. I soon felt like my old self. It was like I was a computer. I just needed to be turned off to reboot.

From the bottom, one can only go up, I started to climb back, much like a staircase with long landings between each step. Two years later, I entered the work force again. This time my position, which I absolutely loved, was as a mental health social worker. The position was at a drop-in center for the homeless. I experienced some great outcomes with my clients. Unknowingly, however, I started to absorb vicarious trauma again. Devastated, once more, I prepared to leave a job I loved. (The funding body didn't see my role as necessary.) Again, the fibro flared and my intense pain became intolerable. I believe the strong pain was from the grief and loss I experienced at not being able to find another social worker position.

My home life in 2017 was strong but brought my husband and I to the same conclusion, that I would not be returning to work. Therefore, we sought a total and permanent disability claim. I was awarded the claim early in 2018.

During this time, I became acutely aware that my father was experiencing elderly abuse. Although Dad and I had a patchy past I wanted to help him. The past, however, did make my resolve difficult. I reasoned with myself that I was a social worker and with my experience we learned to mend our fences between 2017 and 2018. With dad's health failing, we got the news that he was going to be a great grandfather and I a grandmother. Delight and joy filled us both as we awaited the newborn. One week before my grandson was born, my dad passed away. I was at his side. The vision of him passing remains with me when I close my eyes at night.

With the new excitement came grief. My body, again, experienced "hell." After retiring from work my father had become my focus. Now it is my grandson.

Although my grandson is a central focus of my mind and heart, my longing to return to the work I love is a constant. I find I can't seem to commit to anything, because I fear the pain it will cause. Many tell me to use my skills to volunteer, but my heart is still wanting the professional job with the title, respect and acknowledgement that come with it—the networking, professional camaraderie, lunches, drinks after work, humor, holiday celebrations, the whole package. When you've studied for two degrees, are intelligent, and worthy, you want to return to the passion you are filled with. That passion just doesn't disappear overnight. Today I do not have the respect, or identity that I worked for. *How do I move forward, how do I reconcile my grief and loss?* I decided by advocating. I have finally realized I did not waste my time on education because my son and grandson will benefit.

I am still learning to find another life, to accept the loss of my profession as a social worker. This was my identity and is how I think of myself, inside and out. It still makes me sad, feeling in need of help at times, but I will use my positive mindset that seems to help my fibro. I will reset my definition of what my identity is. I will continue to practice meditation, continue to love to create with my crafts, and to immerse myself in card making. While I do these things, I allow my brain to "just be" and that will allow me to be open to what the future holds.

My Battle, My Fight, My Life: Kiwis Can Fly

❧

By Debbie Russell, *New Zealand*

When I put my hand up and decided to write a chapter for this book, I was filled with such mixed emotions: fear, anxiety, and worry about what I should write; what people would say; or if they would judge me. I decided to throw caution to the wind and see what experiences would come out.

I was born in Timaru, October 1968, a normal birth, weighing just over 5lbs, one of five children, four of whom lived. Apparently, I was a sickly child, and ear infections were my biggest problem. I even got abscesses in my ears as they were on the brink of bursting, so I was rushed to Timaru Hospital.

My mum was a stay-at-home mum. She was 16 when she had my older brother. Mum was a strict homemaker, very good at running a clean, tidy home. Even with four children, we were always to stay clean. My dad, a truck driver, was just 17 when they married. He was a black belt in karate and was a big man with a temper. You knew if you got into trouble, you'd be in for a beating. My mum's mom was different. My grandmother was the loveliest, kindest, funniest woman I knew and I adored her! She taught me how to smoke and I continued to smoke most of my life. She died young and grandpa came to live with us.

My parents were always busy with sports. Basketball in the winter, swimming in the summer. I, however, turned my attention to horses. I loved horses and started riding when I was eight or nine years old. I finally got my own pony when I was 13.

We moved away from my birthplace after my grandmother passed, I think I was ten. It was the first time I had ever moved and I found making friends hard.

One Christmas Day, after eating a huge dinner, I was feeling sick so I went to lie down in my grandfather's bedroom. Mum came in and asked if I was okay. I said I had a sore tummy. Dad had followed her in. When Mum left, Dad stayed behind. He said he knew what would make me feel better. He rubbed my tummy then his hand went to my groin, down into my underpants, and said, "Now does that feel better?"

I was too scared to say "NO!" so I said "yes."

"Good, that will be our little secret. Don't tell Mum, it's between us, okay?" Then he walked out. I cried and fell asleep.

From 13-17 years old, my father was having sexual relations with me; my older brother was also raping me until I was 14. When I shared with family friends what was happening with my brother, my mum sent for the doctor so he could tell her if I was still a virgin or not. (*Didn't she believe me?*) I did not tell them about my father because I knew he would kill me if I did.

At 17, I left home to get a job and get away from my father visiting for his pleasure. I was really beginning to hate him.

After starting my job, I met a nice young man, and my adult life began.

Ross was my first husband's name, and right off the bat, we had a miscarriage, then throughout the years three more children. Our relationship was on and off during those years and we moved several times, switching jobs and trying to stay on top of my health problems. Although Ross and I had gotten married, and we had Ashley, Shana Lee, and baby Anita, he continued to be verbally and emotionally abusive and had a very bad temper. That, combined with his controlling nature, made him difficult to deal with. I made the decision to walk away from my husband and girls. It was 1993.

I started the drinking and drugs. Nightclubs became my fix.

I needed to sort things out. I started to take courses, and then the first of many knee surgeries began. I became behind in my course work, and bills began to pile up. Everything was so stressful! I didn't want to go back home to Mum and Dad, as I was ashamed of my debt and that things had gotten out of control, again.

At this time I met Alan, and we became friends. He was much older than I. Alan was 50 and I was 26 but we got along well. Since I felt I needed a new start, Alan and I moved into his son and girlfriend's house. I got a job cleaning at a women's hospital and a parttime job cleaning cars in a yard and showroom. I learned Alan was an alcoholic; he drank beer every night and sometimes would become abusive, not physical, just verbal. My knee problem surfaced again and under a specialist's care, after X-rays, and a CT scan it showed that I had ripped cartilage, ligament, and tendons, and I had trouble with my ACL. Osteoarthritis and more operations followed.

Alan and I moved around quite a bit and along with his drinking, we realized we both had a gambling problem. We continued to have problems but found jobs and became engaged when my divorce came through from Ross. That was in June of 1999.

Throughout these years, my health was up and down with chronic migraines, IBS, lower back pain (from a slipped/bulging disk injury), continued knee problems and I found two lumps on my back. One gave me really sharp stabbing pain around the lump site just on the brink of my buttocks. The excruciating pain made walking a problem and my feet would ache. I had breathing problems that turned out to be COPD, and a blood clot in my lung which kept me in the hospital for some time.

After moving again, this time it was a 10-15 minute walk to get to the main shopping center. One day, I was walking and I had this massive pain in the side of my lower leg near my calf muscle/shin area. I stopped and clasped my leg, crying. My legs and feet were in agony. I couldn't walk. This lady pulled over when she saw something was wrong. She took me back home from just around the corner. That happened a lot over a three-year period. I did talk to my GP but he was unsure what the cause was.

In 2002, Alan found a lump on the side of his neck. It was cancer. The biopsy came back stage four. After surgery, he wasn't prepared for how he'd look and I wasn't either. His smoking had to stop, but he figured out how to continue drinking beer. In 2005, we were back at the hospital for check-ups, the news was not great. It looked like the cancer had spread to his kidneys, liver, and his spine. They tried chemo for three to four months, but it didn't work.

Again, I had decided to work toward a nursing degree, as I had always thought I'd like to become a nurse, so I started my course-work. Then I got notification to have my lumps in my back removed. They biopsied as fatty lumps. They removed two, one on my arm, the other on my back. The one on my back was a lot deeper and larger than they thought. After being discharged, three days later, I returned with chronic pain, twenty-four hours of IV antibiotics and I still had no improvement. They operated again, as I was in chronic pain, and found there was a major abscess and I was about to go into sepsis. I spent nearly three weeks in the hospital. A neurologist came and gave me a piece of paper with a lot of conditions written on it, he thought I had all of those.

Once home, I shifted all my attention to Alan, and put my appointments aside. We liked where we were living then and Alan had a part-time job that he enjoyed, several hours a day. June 2007, we celebrated our wedding anniversary. One morning in early July, it was freezing cold, rain and southerly winds. I asked Alan to stay home because he was still recovering from a chest infection. He decided to go to work anyway and within a couple hours had returned home, unwell. He was admitted into the hospital. Sadly, the infection had turned into pneumonia with a superbug. They said there was noth-ing they could do, it was beyond medical help. Alan decided he wanted to spend his last days at home. My beloved husband died July of 2007.

Not long after Alan's passing, I was lying on the couch crying and the phone rang. It was one of Alan's friends, Wayne. He called to say how sorry he was to hear of Alan's passing. He said he would be interested in having coffee sometime as a friend, so one afternoon we did. That afternoon turned into evening. Laughing and sharing great times of old days of remembrance, our friendship turned into a much deeper level of companionship. Because I was struggling financially, paying off huge amounts of debt, Wayne moved into a spare room as a border. Finances were tight. I got a job at a local service station and took as much work as allowed, being on "Benefit." It still wasn't enough to stop creditors. I never lost any of my household goods, and stuck to agreed payment, I was debt free (mostly in a year) after finding full-time work at a bakery. At that time I was smoking a lot of dope, and drank a small amount of beer.

One day, I had this horrible migraine. Since it was really early in the morning, I called the doctor and explained that I had vomited and my headache was still strong. I had taken pain reliever, but it was not helping. This woman doctor took my blood pressure and it was through the roof. She did some blood work and ordered a CT scan on my head (but told me not to stress out). If the new meds didn't work, come right back. The next few days I hadn't improved much and needed to return. I was placed on a waiting list to see a neurologist.

Then a massive earthquake, 7.1. No one killed. Many after-shocks. My nerves were shot to pieces.

After this, I got my CT scan and waited for the results. Then I was told again that I needed to see that neurologist. The neurologist I saw many years before, who wrote all the things he thought I had on a piece of paper appeared. He told me I believe you have Neurons Disease. He said my migraines were related to my condition and that there was no cure for the condition. He sent me on my way. My regular doctor said that my migraines were just daily chronic ones and nothing about Neuron Disease. I walked out of his appointment even more stressed.

Now another earthquake, 6.4, right under our city; 189 souls lost that day. Over 80 percent of CBD was destroyed. My day of hell. The aftershocks continued for months.

After getting some counseling, hospital appointments for blood conditions, seeing a hematologist, more blood tests ordered and bone marrow biopsy, blood letting done (they take your blood but instead of donating, it's thrown away), my dx: Polycythearmia Rubra Vera. I was told to give up smoking, so I did. Over the next two months, my blood levels returned to normal. Apart from my eyes, I had a twitchy eye, I was seen by an eye specialist and was told it was related to my migraines, not dystonia as my GP thought. My leg pain and walking problems continued.

Over the last few years, I have seen more doctors, specialists, muscle skeleton specialists and two new neurologists, and another general medicine doctor. It was confirmed that I had Fibromyalgia, ME, and chronic fatigue syndrome. The doctors believe the trauma from all the abuse caused PTSD (post-traumatic stress disorder) and this led to my developing the other illnesses. No matter how many appointment's I have, and with whom, I still struggle with chronic pain in my hands, arms, legs and feet. Some days are worse than others. I have been prescribed all kinds of medicines but my list today is smaller than it used to be. Today I try my hardest to get outside and do a bit of exercise, but chronic fatigue pushes my boundaries on how much I can do.

My meds include; Nadolol BP, Fursemide BP. Felodipine (water retention), Betahistine (vertigo), Duolin Inhaler COPD, Patanol (dry eyes), Buspirone (muscle spasm), Docusate sod sennoside (constipation/IBS), Tramadol (pain relief), Panadol/codeine (pain relief), Zopiclone (sleeping), Promethazine (itchy skin).

I also take turmeric capsules and magnesium. I have to watch out for stuff that may interact with my medicines. I found I can't take anti-depressants, they make my heart flutter.

When it comes to food, I have to watch out for certain things. I cannot have: coffee, chocolate, preservatives, sugar, or carbohydrates. I eat mainly red meat, chicken, salmon, fresh veggies, and fruit. I try to stay away from sugary drinks, like juices—especially oranges, because they start my migraines.

Like many other sufferers, I turn to social media to try to find information and support. I do have loved ones that are understanding of my struggle. I need others, however, that understand my pain and the daily battles we fibro patients go through.

There have been many times I thought I was going to die. I've even had those "out of body" moments. Times when I see myself lying on my bed and I fly through the house elevating toward the heavens.

The thing that compels me to keep fighting and keep my faith is the hope that one day we will all have a cure. A cure for Fibro, ME, chronic fatigue. I pray the doctors find the reasons why our bodies hurt and make us suffer like we do.

I would like to dedicate this chapter to someone who has been with me the last 11 years since Alan passed away. Wayne has been my tower of strength, and encouraged me on my worse days. He has looked after me when I didn't even have the energy to look after myself. He has been my voice when I could not speak, and he has shown me what true love is. He just keeps giving and never asked for anything in return. When the news broke about my dad having sexually abused my niece, Tia, I was lying on the couch crying. I was so sick with all the stress. I knew Wayne understood how I was feeling because he got up, went to the bedroom and returned with a book. That book was given to him as a wedding present. He placed it on my chest and said I want you to have this. I believe you need it more than I do. The book was *The Bible*, his King James Version. I want you to find a church to go to because I want the best for you. I said I always wanted to go to that Salvation Army just around the corner from us. I promised that day I would go. So I did.

Today, four years later, I am an Adherent Soldier of the Salvation Army. I was baptized two years ago. I have been blessed with a wonderful church family made of many new friends. My life is new in every way. I am smoke-free nearly three years next April. Dope-free about two years. I don't drink alcohol, and I am a grandmother of four beautiful grandchildren who I adore. I am proud of my girls who strive to levels I never tried to reach. Each of them are perfect in my eyes. They are warm, loving, caring women.

I give praise to my Saviour, Lord Jesus Christ. Jesus brings me healing and a new life. I am in his hands and he will guide me through the valley and bring me home when the time comes. Until then I must fly. *Kiwis really do fly.*

Today this Kiwi girl is flying. Flying to new heights and not letting things like sexual and emotional abuse, fibromyalgia, PRV, ME, COPD, IBS, vertigo or migraines rule her life. Doctors and the medical field will remain but they will not rule me anymore!

The Beginning, The Middle, And Not Quite The End...

By Ann Scollins

The Beginning...

Hmm! The beginning is, I would assume, on the date of my birth. But that is a whole different story! This story is about *fibromyalgia* and the many other medical conditions that go along with it. I believe my fibro diagnosis came about because of so many things happening to my body when I hit my late thirties. I remember going for a checkup with my primary care doctor and my blood work revealed a problem with my thyroid. *That test necessitated other tests, of course!* So off I went for some type of nuclear test. I recall lying on the table and a large machine suspended from the ceiling passed over me.

Then, I was sent to get an MRI (closed one at that time) of my thyroid. Both, with and without contrast. Not a pleasant experience! First, I was in that horrid tube listening to the loud booming noises and almost immediately began to feel very uncomfortable and claustrophobic. This part lasted about 40 minutes and I was very happy to finally have my body rolled out of the machine. *But, not over yet!* Had to have an IV put into my almost nonexistent veins in my arm. *HA! HA! After several attempts, there was a success!* Back into the MRI for another 40 minutes. Upon exiting the machine, my head was throbbing, my arm was bleeding (after removal of the IV) and my body was shaking. I don't drive, so I use public transportation. When I was getting ready to leave, the receptionist must have noticed my discomfort and called a taxi for me to be taken home at their expense! *Thank you!*

The last test for my thyroid was to see an ENT Specialist. He put a scope up my nose and down my throat to visualize the thyroid and my voice box. Finally, it was time to see my primary care doctor for the results. The diagnosis: Hashimoto's Hypothyroidism. This is an autoimmune condition resulting in the thyroid gland not producing enough thyroid hormone. I was placed on Synthroid, a synthetic form of the hormone that I was deficient in. I was also informed I would need to have blood work done every six months to check my thyroid levels and to have my medication adjusted if necessary. Bloodwork and medication is required for the rest of my life.

The Middle...

I've always had extremely heavy menstrual cycles and by my 40's things were worsening. I was placed on birth control pills! *They were supposed to help but believe me, they never did!* Towards the end of my 40's, I found a great OB/GYN, as I was fed up with the current one and his birth control pills! *But I digress.* Around 47 I had started to experience a lot of strange feelings. Just worried and anxious all the time. My stomach was giving me lots of problems. Gas, bloating, feeling like I was hungry, yet couldn't eat. One day it was so bad, I took myself to the ER and after an X-ray ended up with a nasogastric tube to create suction in my stomach as the X-ray indicated some sort of blockage. *I might need surgery!* My primary doctor came along with a surgeon. He had another X-ray taken and it showed a lessening of whatever had shown in the previous one! Out came the nasogastric tube. I was given an appointment to see him in his office. That appointment led to a laparoscopic procedure scheduled the following week—as an inpatient—to see if there were any adhesions, as these do not show up on X-rays or CT scans. There was a small circular adhesion from a prior appendectomy on my 27th birthday. He thought perhaps my bowel was slipping into and out of the space in the center of the adhesion. Took several weeks of healing before I returned to work.

The following year these same symptoms returned but they were even more pronounced and after many exams and surgical consults I said, "NO!" emphatically, "NO!" to an open surgery of my abdomen. My gut feeling made me think there was no blockage; all this was something else! It turned out that all of this was being caused by anxiety. The anxiety of unknown cause. That was what started me on my way to the diagnosis of fibro. It took some time but I was now 51, recently separated from my husband of 29 years *(at my request)*. I was experiencing horrible pain in front part of my thighs. Can only describe that pain as someone wringing the water out of a very wet towel by hand.

My primary doctor did blood work and my ANA level came back as positive. It was very high. It is written as a ratio. Normal is 1:<40; mine was 1:620! Off to a rheumatologist for further testing and I do mean testing! *I didn't know there were that many blood tests on this planet!* After the tests were all completed, which took a couple of months, he diagnosed me with fibromyalgia. He started me on my first course of medications. Many different medications were tried and many failed, mostly due to side effects which I could not tolerate. In my younger days, I never had any side effects from any medications! There was Amitriptyline, Nortriptyline, Xanax, Ambien, Mobic, Celebrex; might have been more, but these I remember! My symptoms were actually getting worse each time I visited this rheumatologist and he eventually dismissed me saying, "There's no more I can do for you!" *That was the best thing because I was forgetting to do everyday tasks at work. My mind was in a constant whirl!* I moved on to a psychiatrist because my anxiety was getting worse. We also tried different medications at that time; Paxil, Lexapro, and finally, Cymbalta. He felt that because of my chronic pain and because of the past several years of surgeries (Note: I had a total hysterectomy the month before I turned 50!) that the fear of the unknown was legitimately causing my reactions. I also had a critical splenic hemorrhage after a routine colonoscopy when I was 51. I was in ICU for four days and in the Step-Down Unit for two days. Luckily, my spleen closed up on its own and I did not need surgical removal of it. We finally settled on just Xanax which allowed me some better sleep (Alprazolam in its generic form). I had been awakening in the middle of the night shaking, crying and feeling terrified. This is how my panic disorder presented itself and Alprazolam is what helped!

At this same time, I was seeing a neurologist for my fibro because I was also having balance issues. Further blood work was indicative now of a diagnosis of mixed connective tissue disorder *(or maybe MS!)* My MCTD diagnosis indicated some positives for both Lupus and CREST form of Scleroderma. However, I am missing one of the factors needed to definitely indicate Lupus. Thus, it is MCTD, and I am missing two of the factors for CREST an MRI of my brain showed a lacunar infarction in mid-brain (having lost my balance several times one night when I got up to use the bathroom) once mentioned to the rheumatologist, it was deemed a "sleepwalking" episode from Ambien. I stopped taking it immediately. It was now believed to have been a type of stroke, which did not leave me with any paralysis or other problems.

Not Quite the End ...

I am now 70! I live in another state from where I was born, raised, married, and raised my own children. I only see a primary physician and he prescribes the Synthroid, Hypertension meds, Alprazolam, Flexeril, and any other meds I need, like antibiotics. I no longer see a rheumatologist. It was found that I had a nodule in my middle lobe of the right lung just one year after moving here. CTs and PET scans were indicative of cancer, but a bronchoscopy was negative and a needle biopsy showed "granulomatous inflammation." The thoracic surgeon I see believes I might have aspirated something and my autoimmune system sent out antibodies to surround it, which lodged in my lung. I am currently being followed by CT scans and visits to him for the results of same. CT scan last done in November 2018. It showed the nodule, slightly larger. Next CT scan is in March 2019. It will make one year since this was initially discovered and the traumas to my body and the thought of lung cancer (which my mom passed from 36 years ago at the age of 65, three weeks after her diagnosis), has exacerbated my fibro and especially my fatigue.

I am now seeing an interventional pain management doctor for injections, taking Tai Chi classes and I take my medications judiciously. Other than Tramadol, which I was prescribed many years ago, I have never taken pain medications/opioids for my fibro pain. Now when my pain from herniated discs in both lumbar and cervical spine act up, I use a soft collar in which to sleep, put on lidocaine patches or rub the area with lidocaine cream and take a Flexeril before bed. I do that after I take my glaucoma eye drops. I have mild glaucoma in one eye, but both get treated! Yes, I have a lot going on. I have made new friends and despite all, I am feeling blessed!

So again, it is not quite the end...

I Won't Surrender

By Eugenia Volino

A school does not prepare you for everything that can happen in life. Most people do not think anything bad is going to happen to them. That is why personal injury lawyers barrage our televisions with commercials 24/7, 365. Have you ever noticed how many times during your television show a commercial for slips and falls, workplace and car accident, bankruptcy and Social Security lawyer commercials come on? I bet you are totally oblivious to them by now, but if you are one of the millions of unfortunate souls that have had their life altered because of some injury, mishap or medical condition these commercials resonate if not torture you. Let us not forget the commercial for the "miracle drugs" that are supposed to cure and make our medical conditions disappear while the depiction of the people in the commercials make our diseases look like a mild inconvenience at best.

You live your life right and proper. Watch your weight; stay physically fit with sports or some athletic endeavor. Work hard to provide a good quality of life for yourself and possibly your family. You mind your business, keep your temper in check, and as the saying goes, "keep your nose clean." Then by no fault of your own tragedy strikes. In my case, it was a car accident that required the "jaws of life" to remove me from the car and then be flown to the nearest medical center. Terrified is an understatement. Your life as you knew it has completely and forever been changed. The insurance companies take over your life. The average person, being naïve, does not realize what torture awaits them. Especially when it's your insurance that you have paid in to for years. (Never do you ever think they would be against you.)

Now if you are unlucky enough to have been hurt at work, the nightmare is even more ferocious. It wasn't your fault you were just doing your job, why would your employer be unsupportive and not help fix your health? First, to survive the mess of insurance do not think with your logical brain, they are there to keep as much money for the insurance company as possible. Second, the insurance company is not on your side. This is a falsehood. Insurance is not there to fix you if *THEY* have to pay for it. Believe me that was a "hard pill for me to swallow."

You are probably thinking what makes me such an expert, she is just bitter and wants to complain. I can tell you that I have had the experience of a lifetime! First, I am a victim of many car accidents, which has altered my life forever. I've also slipped/fallen. That finished me off so to speak. I have survived the ins and outs of social security disability (four-year battle) and have the experience of working ten years as a workers comp/personal injury paralegal (for the injured person). Lastly, I have one year experience as a social security disability paralegal.

With human experience and work experience I have been on and seen both sides of this world we call "Living or Surviving with Chronic Pain caused by XYZ." No matter what name you call your medical condition, once it leaves the world of acute, curable or fixable and enters the world of chronic, confusing, incurable or unfixable your world no longer makes sense. You are now treated callously by both insurance companies, doctors, and the world. You are no longer a viable productive citizen, therefore, you are now considered a problem.

Insurance companies see you as a drain on their pockets, the doctors see you like a mystery they can't fix. So the answer? They don't want to be bothered by you at all. Society and loved ones look at you as a drain on their time also. They don't see the "before you," only the "after fibro you" (which is an oddity and who wants to associate with that). If you have a terminal illness the world opens its arms to you, doctors go out of there way for you, some even have fundraisers. Why? Maybe because curable or not there is an expiration date on when the fuss will end. (It isn't proper etiquette to turn your back on someone with a terminal/fatal disease.)

Let me give a little background on me. I was living my life working two jobs. Both jobs were very physical and between the two, I worked about 50-60 hours a week. I was raising my almost ten-year-old daughter, with my husband who only worked one job. I stayed physically active with my daughter roller-skating, playing basketball, tennis, and other fun outdoor sports. My marriage was not a happy one, but I believed in "till death do you part" so I stayed and dealt with it. We had a modest home, we went on small weekend vacations, had two vehicles, and our daughter was in various after school activities. We were classified as middle class.

My life was far from sedentary. I had just turned 30 and my daughter was turning ten, naturally like most parents that work too much, I wanted to spoil her and give her a tenth birthday she wouldn't forget, after all, this was a double digit birthday and I wanted it to be memorable. I planned an out of town roller skating party for her and her friends. Sadly, fate had other ideas for us. I was driving on unfamiliar roads with my daughter in the front seat with her birthday cake on her lap. Her dad was in the car directly behind us trying to pick up a few of the children for today's festivities. I was approaching a hill going 45mph and I had the car on cruise control. As I was descending the hill, I saw a stop sign in front of me, it had been obstructed by a low hanging tree branch so I did not see it at the top of the hill or I would have adjusted my speed. The road was now crossing a major highway that was prone to truck traffic, how I wasn't killed still remains a mystery to us. Now we all know that you cannot stop on a dime. I won't bother with the details. We went through that stop sign.

After staying in the hospital a week, I was sent home on crutches with the diagnosis of "damaged." Broken bones heal, soft tissue does not. This was the start of my experience with accident insurance. Years later, I learned that I indeed could have sued the county for poor placement of a crucial sign. I hired a lawyer but he didn't want to make waves with the county. My accident did result in proper signage. This did not help me, however.

I went to a specialist who ran many tests on me; after all they had the insurance money to spend! I was put on various drugs and treatments. I tried everything that was requested of me. I wanted my life back. I had become completely reliant on my husband at the time. I couldn't sit, stand or walk for more than 15 minutes without severe pain. I had horrible brain fog, unrelenting fatigue and insomnia. I felt like I was dying slowly. I even saw a psychiatrist who diagnosed me with severe PTSD. I wouldn't drive a car and shook uncontrollably even as a passenger. My freedom and carefree nature was gone. I cried all the time and I was diagnosed with, related depression and anxiety. (More drugs/therapy.)

My specialist, after ruling out any major diseases, told me to try biofeedback which I did and that didn't help. My therapist tried to hypnotize me but my subconscious didn't allow it. Slowly I was losing hope, then the bomb came. My car insurance sent me a check for $243, which was my final "lost wages reimbursement." I made more than $243 a week, so I was mortified! I called the insurance company and they informed me that the money on the policy was gone. You see medical expenses come out of "lost wage reimbursement." Every drug, test, treatment drained my policy. (It had been only a year.) *Now, what do I do?*

I was told I should have been trying for social security disability the whole time. No one had told me that. They sent a back to work counselor to my home who even though I couldn't sit, stand, or walk for more than 15 minutes, he sent my (before the accident) resume to various employers to help me find work. I found this out when an employer called me, offering me an awesome position that the before me would have jumped at. I had to turn it down, however, explaining my circumstances as I hung up the phone crying. I was furious at what that counselor had done, without my permission, without common sense, without even telling me he had sent my old resume to employers. I called the insurance company and reported him, they apologized stating he shouldn't have done. *How does that help me?*

My depression deepened, I felt useless. In devastation and despair I ate to comfort myself, after all, I had no control over anything else in my life except what I put in my mouth. My husband wasn't happy about this nor was he happy I was still walking on crutches. He was livid that he had to be the sole provider, he was used to me working two jobs totaling three salaries, now he was bitter and enraged all the time. I had finally started driving, so he didn't have to take me to any more doctors or appointments. Driving out of town or on major highways still terrified me so I still needed rides for those appointments. I started the SSDI process as I was told but I had no clue that would be a nightmare in itself. Once the insurance money stopped so did my specialist. He washed his hands of me stating "he did all that he could" and released me to my primary. A doctor who treats you for the flu or ear infections has no clue how to treat "soft tissue damage and PTSD." He did his best as that is all my insurance would cover. No more tests, just medication, I felt like a human guinea pig.

I was on antidepressants that made me fat and did nothing for the depression, anxiety, or sleep. I took sleeping pills that made me a walking zombie in the morning and only gave me a few hours of sleep at night. I did physical therapy, and after a few years I still walked with a cane. After going to another specialist, I graduated to a Canadian Crutch to keep my wrists straight because I developed wrist complications.

I went to a "pain specialist" who promised me a cure with these magical "epidural cortisone steroid injections" delivered directly into my spine. I researched this injection and it can bring on fibromyalgia or make it a hundred times worse. Cortisone steroids take years to leave the body, I had six of them. After six weeks of hell, my back was a hundred times worse and my neck which was a mild issue was now full-blown pain 24/7. I was livid that he did this to me, then he had the gall to suggest acupuncture! My medical insurance questioned every treatment, every procedure, yet doctors find a way to get everything approved. I was nothing but a guinea pig. Meanwhile, all this hell was taking place in my body, SSDI was taking their sweet time with my application. Our family income quickly went from having three paychecks to only one, this was a direct hit and we lost everything. We had to file bankruptcy. To add insult to injury, we had to go live with my parents (not the greatest environment for my psyche). When the denial from SSDI came (I found out later that they usually turn everyone down the first time) I didn't know where to turn. I was so lost and I didn't know what I did in my past lives to deserve this hell now.

I went to my primary care doctor and demanded that they send me to a specialist who knows what they're doing because SSDI says there is nothing wrong with me. They sent me to a rheumatologist who ran more tests and then the dreaded "Trigger Point" test that nearly knocked me out from the pain. I finally had a doctor who knew what she was doing, or so I thought. She callously told me that she had "good news and bad news." The "good news" was that I wasn't going to die (that's good even though I had been praying for death daily), "the bad news was that there is *NO CURE.*" I was shocked, amazed, dumbfounded, and speechless. She told me that I had a condition called fibromyalgia and no one knows what causes it or how to cure it. This was *not* the answer I wanted. I wanted a diagnosis that could be cured and pronounced. She put me on an experimental treatment which was an anti-malaria drug and it nearly hospitalized me. Frustrated, she released me to my primary care doctor to continue doing what they were doing (nothing). Again, the medical community washed their hands of me. Thankfully, my primary did not, but all I got was more antidepressants and sleeping meds. We never reached into the pain pill arena, as I was terrified, I would become addicted. I am adopted and do not know what I am predisposed to. I lived on Ibuprofen though, muscle relaxers and Neurontin, which is supposed to treat fibro.

Meanwhile, I retained a paralegal from a nonprofit agency to fight my SSDI battle; fortunately, she had filed the paperwork for my appeal before my diagnosis of fibro. It had been four years since my car accident, four years of hell, despair, and isolation. My body was no longer mine it had a mind of its own from minute to minute, 365 days a year, and 24/7 *PAIN!* I just wanted it to end. Sadly, the diagnosis of fibro did not save me. If anything, it hindered me even more because no one believed it was a real condition. It wasn't even a disease but a syndrome, that word has such a negative connotation, what does that even mean syndrome?

Well, I can tell you this, when my husband at the time, since divorced, heard my diagnosis all the loving care and understanding went right out the window. He looked at me as a fake or a phony someone who just did not want to work or do housework. *Yep, that is right, I was just a plain ole phony, I choose to destroy my life, I choose to be in pain 24/7, 365 days a year. I choose to ruin my promising career as a hotel sales manager. I choose to stop being able to roller-skate with my daughter, play tennis, ride a bike (I haven't ridden a bike in 23+years, stationary bike doesn't count) and so many more activities. I can't even state them all because it would be another page. I choose to lose my friends because they could not handle me not being the fun outgoing spontaneous person I used to be. I choose to not be able to sleep at night and be exhausted all day. I choose to barely exist, that's right I choose it all, wouldn't you?* Sadly, this became my life and I had to justify my condition to everyone. I had to justify my use of a Canadian Crutch when I didn't have MS. I had to justify why I had to push a special chair around the college so I could attend my classes.

One good thing came from this, I qualified for SSDI and that also qualified me for assistance through a government agency, called VESID. I was able to go back to school to get retrained in a field I could do. After many tests and research, I decided to try to qualify for college to get an associate's degree and become a paralegal. The program was highly competitive and I didn't know if I had the ability. My brain was so foggy from fatigue. I tested and I was accepted. I was shocked when I got the approval letter from the college.

Then I had to get the approval from the agency. I did and I was all set for the first day of college. My husband at the time was *not* happy, his family, and my family all thought it was so stupid for me to risk losing my SSDI by going to college when I can just sit at home the rest of my life. (I was only 34 and collect my disability. A whopping $650/month. My daughter got $300/month whoop-de-doo.) I told them I wasn't a quitter and that I was too young to be done with life.

Against my husband's wishes, I went to college. It was very difficult to sit in class through lectures. My body was aching from the hardness of the seats, so I would bring pillows to sit on. Although I was only 34, I felt soooo much older. Especially with the cane. But VESID came through for me. They had me run tests on what adaptive equipment I needed to help me get through school. I got a desktop computer for home to type my papers, voice-activated software, but I talked faster than it could type, special pens, a footrest, but most importantly a chair that supported my complete body, right to the tip of my head. It was on wheels, so I had to push it all over college but it helped me sit in class. Later, after I graduated, it even helped me at work. To keep everything after graduation all I had to do was retain a job within a year of graduation. Easy, right? Not really, it took five years to get through a two year program because I had to start very slow with only one class per semester then the following year, I upped it to two classes. Finally, by my fourth year I was a full-time student.

With all these class hours comes a lot of homework so that was another reason it took so long to graduate, I watched two classes graduate before me. The only great thing was that my daughter and I would do our homework together, she was in junior high school when I started. I graduated with my associate's degree the same year she graduated from high school. She was my cheer-leader for the whole five years. She was so proud of what her momma was accomplishing even though I was suffering. She heard me cry at night and in the morning, she would help with the chores so I could study. My daughter was my rock, my world. My husband, who should have been my rock was the opposite of supportive. He wasn't even at my graduation, he was working.

I justified myself daily for years to everyone because when I told people what I had they would look at me like I was speaking a foreign language or was an alien. Although I justified myself, there were the constant doubters. I spoke with my professor often about my doubts. I wondered if I could be anything or if I was wasting my time, who would hire me? She told me that "if I could get through this program and graduate that would be proof enough for any employer." I struggled, but I did graduate in 2002. After graduation, because of my PTSD (something else no one believed I had), I couldn't drive out of town for a job and that's where all the law offices were. The law offices in my hometown used their secretaries as there "paralegal" why not? They can pay them less, so finding a job was very hard. The fighter in me wouldn't give up. I had my associate's degree and I was determined I would get a job. Once again, no support from anyone, except my daughter who was in college herself now, they all thought it was stupid and unnecessary after all.

I found a job as a substitute teacher, which worked great because they would call in the morning and if you didn't want to work you just didn't answer the phone. I started off slow at first but within a year, I was working almost every day. I was happy, fulfilled, and wishing I had become a teacher instead. My family thought it was stupid and a waste of time because the pay was so trivial. I still had my SSDI because I didn't make enough to be kicked off it. I felt fulfilled, I still walked with a cane and had very painful days but the kids, teachers and schools accepted me and that was good enough for me.

Meanwhile, I kept my eyes out for the paralegal job I wanted, preferably in Social Security or personal injury because I wanted to help people and make a difference. My dream finally came through, almost three years after I graduated. I found a part-time job as a paralegal/legal assistant for a one man office that dealt in workers comp mostly. Personal injury was the main focus of the main firm in the city—but our satellite office was comp. I did, however, take intakes for personal injury clients when they called our office. The small satellite office that we started grew quickly and it was necessary for me to go full time or become a file clerk, so I decided to bite the bullet and go for it.

My education blossomed, I dealt with many different kinds of people, from many different careers that were devastated by an unplanned life-changing injury. Boy, could I relate! No one knew about my illness, I kept it a secret. I didn't want them to know until I proved myself. After a year, I finally told my boss, my pain levels were increasing daily and I needed more help. Being a one man office it created a lot of responsibility for me. I typed 40 percent of my day, talked on the phone with clients, doctors, nurses, insurance carriers, and even lawyers and the occasional judges another 30 percent of my day. I read medical reports and filed for 20 percent of my day, and for the other ten percent of my day, I prepared the files for court. I was exhausted and my work was falling behind. He understood and promised me a file clerk position but one never came. He did not fault me, even though my illness had caused a decrease in my job performance, he was actually impressed with everything I could do. Unless it was a major legal issue, I handled most of the clients. He used to say that I could do his job. I so wish life had turned out differently for me, I could have been a kick ass lawyer. However, as the person with the most contact with these forlorn clients, I helped a lot of people. When I read medical reports that stated the clients were malingering or exaggerating symptoms, I would let the lawyer know so he could confront them. He would insist on clarification from the patient's doctor asking what was going on? If it was true, he would try to snap them into reality and let them know that it could cost them their benefits. People don't realize that when you are on workers comp, insurance companies are for the employer (not the employee). They watch their cases with a fine tooth comb and if there is a chance that they can kick you off of your biweekly benefits, you better believe they would. This would result in the need for a hearing to prove them wrong.

In the ten years I worked at that firm I saw so many people's lives destroyed by just what a doctor's report had said. This is true for Social Security as well, when you are preparing a case, which I also had the opportunity to do in my internship with a nonprofit agency while in college, you have to be ever so careful with every report. You have to pick the report apart and see if there are any red flag words in it. The word syndrome is a big red flag. There were so many syndromes now besides fibro. There was Myofascial pain syndrome, complex regional pain disorder just to name a few—when these appeared, the case was doomed. Be it workers comp or social security, the insurance companies, and the government agency now can say it's a syndrome, what is it? What is the cure for it? Most importantly what caused it? I saw normal everyday hardworking people turn into shells of who they were. Many lost their homes, boats, cars, marriages because the toll their injury has caused. Many were depressed, hooked on pain meds, and some just withered away. It was a very depressing job, but when I had the opportunity, I used myself as an example (as a third person) to give people who would listen the scenario that life could work out. Many took my advice and checked in to retraining programs, some started new lives. I know I talked several people down from the edge of the cliff and kept them from jumping, that was so fulfilling (helping others).

Neurontin, two different antidepressants, muscle relaxers, and Darvon (until they took it off the market) then hydrocodone when it got bad, controlled my fibro so I could work. I couldn't take several of these during the day or my brain fog would be exacerbated. So I would double up on them after work, and I was mostly like a zombie at home but I still took my dog for a walk every night. Weekends were spent recuperating so my quality of life was not great but while I was at work, I wasn't the girl with the syndrome. I was the girl with the answers and that made all the difference in the world.

Sadly, it didn't last. I had a worker's comp injury of my own, severe carpal tunnel syndrome (another syndrome) in my right hand that sidelined me for longer than it should have, thanks to fibro. What should have been two months of recovery took four months. Then when I was ready to return to work, I was walking my dog and tripped over her, smashing my knee into a concrete sidewalk, tearing my Meniscus, so I had to have surgery. All this stress was making my fibro kick my butt on a daily basis. Not to mention the work related migraines that started five years ago. After surgery, while recovering a day later I fell down a flight of stairs at home and smashed into my washer and dryer on top of each other, so basically a brick wall. Ended up with even worse neck issues, back and now I have a concussion. *Lucky, lucky me.* Sadly, the office couldn't keep using a temp and I lost my job, once again my career that I worked so hard for was gone.

I learned a lot in my years at the firm, so I did contact insurance companies to find out if I had out of work coverage and found out that the insurance my job had was for guests getting hurt and not employees. I couldn't sue the landlord because I didn't want to lose my home, with a dog, it was hard to find a good place to live. I did, however, contact Social Security and within four months, my benefits were turned back on at a higher rate because I had worked a higher paying job for ten years. We only ran short of money for a few months. Catching up, however, would not be easy.

You see, over the last 23 years, my life has changed numerous times. I had to file bankruptcy twice, lost two homes at different junctures in time. Finally, I downsized into a small apartment and had to purge a lot of belongings. When my husband finally left me for a healthy woman (four years older than me) I was devastated and lost. I had to downsize even more and relocate, all because of this damn syndrome. No matter how hard I tried the syndrome was constantly destroying my life. Each time it changed I would have to go through the stages of grief: first, denial; second, anger; third, bargaining; fourth, depression; fifth, acceptance. Over and over through the years I've had to go through this grief. Then of course after grieving, would come reinventing…but I think this wasn't in the cards for me this last time, my concussion wasn't going away and I was showing signs of early dementia. I was only 48, this could not be happening to me! But again, being adopted I had no clue if I was predisposed. Needless to say, after much testing my results were inconclusive and again, I had a syndrome. This was a good one, I had concussion syndrome. Seriously, enough with the syndromes!

This was the final blow to my marriage but I was ok because he was a horrible person and I devoted 27 years of my life to him in which twenty of it had been with fibro. I did finally, rid myself of my cane while I was in college thanks to perseverance and physical therapy. Now I have it back thanks to my fall. I felt useless again, and no support from home didn't help. My daughter was supportive but she lived several miles away. I was a broken person inside and out and apparently hubby had dealt with enough. He left me in a financial mess with no money except my SSDI, bills to pay and rent. I had no choice but to start over somewhere else. My daughter let me room with her for a while but her roommate and I did not click so I had to leave. I had received no help for my concussion syndrome due to my lousy insurance so my brain was recuperating only with the help of me. Needless to say, I wasn't doing the best job. The fibro was exacerbating everything and made it hard to move by now and the doctors had added Valium to my list of drugs…my weight dropped quickly from the disruption to my life. I found an apartment that would allow my dog. I now entered into a new nightmare…public assistance.

For years people told me to leave my husband, but I didn't think I could afford to live alone and that was when I was working how could I do it now on just SSDI? They told me a fairy tale; you will get so much help. Food stamps, rent assistance, utilities etc. you will be taken care of. I call it a fairy tale because that was not the case. Even though I was on disability, was all alone, the cost of living was lower in NYS and I still made $100 too much. I did not get any help whatsoever. No rental assistance, no utilities, and no medical insurance. My SSDI had to cover everything and the rental prices were high in my area where I was able to live with a dog. They did finally agree to give me a whopping $12 per month for Food Stamps (wow I guess I don't get much to eat). I lived on peanut butter, tuna fish, mac & cheese and whatever else I could get from the food banks. I had fallen so far, you better believe my fibro was kicking my butt on a daily basis. The husband disappeared after quitting his lucrative job so he didn't have to get nailed for alimony. He finally reappeared a year later in Florida, so my divorce was useless I didn't get one penny for the hell I endured for 27 years. He had finally won, but I was free from his tyranny so I felt I had won.

I almost died six months prior because I had lost so much weight due to being overmedicated and it nearly sent me into a stroke. Luckily my daughter came to check on me as I asked her to come to walk the dog as I wasn't feeling well. When she arrived she found me unresponsive and very cold. She was a nurse by now, yes, living with me all those years made her grow up fast but also made her kind and compassionate and she went into the medical field later in life. Thankfully, for me she did, she knew exactly what to do. After a week in the hospital, convincing the psych team that I did not do this on purpose, I finally was sent home. It took a month to recover from this episode. Numerous times throughout this life with fibro and other medical issues I just wanted to give up, end it all, so many times I wanted to just go to sleep and never wake up. Now being that

I came so close to having that come true, I now know I do not want to die. The hospital took me off all my medications cold turkey and after a month, I only went back on three of those medications: my stomach pill, my antidepressant, and Neurontin, but at a much lower dose. No more muscle relaxers or Valium, no more pain meds. I was now living with my pain and trying to accept it.

I also decided that it was time I took back my life, I was tired of barely surviving, I had absolutely no quality of life. I got involved with a social organization that was very diverse with many opportunities to do stuff and a lot of it was for free. I also started dating, online was the only way to find men my age. I found that if you were honest and upfront with them right at the beginning, you were set up for failure. Fibro is a lot to handle, add concussion syndrome and the date is over. I had a lot of first dates but not too many second ones. This was fine because I had a lot to give the right person. I was in no hurry, I was trying to fix my life once again and reinvent myself.

I found a part time job—I figured after being out of work for three years and having the memory issues being a cashier in a department store was all I could handle. I did a great job and now had money for proper nutrition. I branched out to taking supplements. I had tried all of them years ago, I thought why not give it a shot? I tried Reiki, which was amazing when it was happening but the price was prohibitive on a regular basis. Slowly, my body was adapting to working on a regular basis and even my brain was improving, probably from the repetition. After six months my body started showing signs of extreme strain, I had to cut my hours, which then caused me to cut down on my extras like supplements. After two years, I finally had to quit because on top of the fibro and degenerative knees I now had a bulging disc in my back and a herniated disc. Physical therapy was not helping, it was a combination of the fibro hindering my healing and my work. So I had to quit. Luckily by now I was in a loving committed relationship and he asked me and my dog to move in with him and his 15 year-old son. I was shocked. I did say yes and was in *love*. He is so caring, and understanding of my fibro, migraines, back, knees, neck, etc. so I decided to reinvent myself again.

I WON'T SURRENDER

For four months my fibro excessively raged 24/7. I was no longer able to control it with my "bite the bullet" attitude. So I withdrew and fell back into my old patterns of isolation and sleeping. I only had SSDI for an income so expensive treatments were out. I didn't expect my guy to pay for them. I lost the ability to go to food banks where I did get salmon, tilapia and tuna fish a lot, so I started to gain back some of the weight I had lost three years prior. My health was actually getting way worse. Yet I was happy so why was that happening. They say that fibro is fed by stress... I have fed that monster inside me for years, so why now that I was happy, was I was getting worse? I wasn't happy because I wasn't working, I just didn't want to accept it. I was in the five stages of grief again grieving not for being in a loving relationship but grieving for losing my independence and self-reliance I fought so hard to achieve. Grieving for the body I had mastered control over last year. Grieving for more than I could even imagine. Grieving for the what ifs, would haves, could haves, should haves over and over through the last 23 years. It was time to stop.

A few months ago I started on a wellness plan that finally changed my life for the last time, my diet. I now was entering down a road that was so confusing and contradicting to everything I ever was taught or learned. But I figured, what did I have to lose? I started a keto diet, which is basically 70 percent healthy fat, 20 percent protein, and ten percent non-starchy carbs. I also started with new supplements, one being a bullet coffee. Not only did I lose weight I started feeling better, stronger, and less fatigue. Then I started using a few different special supplements which had pure organic vitamins and minerals in them not only was I feeling stronger but I was hurting less in my joints. (The one supplement has glucosamine chondroitin, turmeric, magnesium, etc.) the other supplement was taking care of my stress. My fog was lifting and I could actually see the light at the end of the tunnel.

I took a chance and applied for a legal assistant job and *poof* two interviews later, I got it! It's only part-time but it's *work* and it makes me feel useful and it supplements my SSDI. So now I can afford to take care of me again. My body is taking a hit again, all the typing I do is killing my neck and arms which triggers my migraines and

139

aggravates my fibro. I keep plugging along and it helps that I have a guy who cares and leaves me alone when I want isolation to recover. If it wasn't for the barking dogs we have I would probably recover a lot quicker. I still cancel on people, plans have to be shelved for another time but the difference is I know it isn't forever this time.

What made me want to write this chapter started out as "Here's My Journey" turned into "I Won't Surrender." Then while I was at work the boss asked me to outline Medical for a car accident case, we had a problem. I could handle that I've done it a million times. While I was outlining the Medical the words *exaggeration of symptoms* appeared. I knew that the case was lost. Unless the insurance company has a lousy lawyer which they never do or that they settle before this ever hits a judge. The more I read the more I saw all the mistakes she had made. First, was not going to the hospital immediately after the accident. Second, was just having her primary care doctor treat her—they were over medicating and misdiagnosing. Third, she took almost a year to get to a specialist. Fourth, she wasn't noticing the doctors, chiropractors, and physical therapists document everything you say and do in their office. Fifth, she didn't understanding that the insurance doctors (IMEs) there were supposed to be independent but they were paid for by the insurance company! When I saw these reports, I saw that people need to be educated before something happens to them either by an injury, accident or illness. They need to know how to protect themselves from doubt and ridicule. So this is my attempt at that.

When you go to an SSDI hearing be prepared for embarrassing questions, but don't be afraid to stand your ground. A perfect example: greeters at Walmart if you can sit, stand or walk then you can work…really well let's see. I can only sit for an x amount of time, I can only stand for an x amount of time, I can only walk for an x amount of time, give them the minutes and make sure you have medical reports to back that up. Even work from home jobs are difficult to do if you can't handle staring at a monitor without getting a migraine, resulting in having to lay down. You need to be *EXACT* and *CANDID* with your doctors because they will document *ALL* in their reports, then when the time comes no one can question if you are malingering or exaggerating your symptoms.

Having fibro has been 23 years of life altering, painstaking, exhausting terror for it feels that I am a spectator in my own body and it all depends on the path the monster within you wants to take. My life changes minute to minute, hour to hour, day to day, to a week, to a month. Plans? Why make them they'll just be taken away. Yes, I grieve a lot but I also learned that determination and refusal to let this syndrome win will make you handle this life that was given to you. *Just understand that pain is subjective and* only you know *what that means to you.*

I don't try to please anyone anymore. I just take it day by day, when my plans get canceled, I grieve for a while worrying if this is the end again for me, but I try to get through the stages quicker, recuperate and move on. My advice to anyone going through this life…our minds and bodies can adapt, you just have to be persistent and insistent with it. Remember you are a warrior and warriors don't quit or surrender.

I wake up every day hoping that I will be able to handle everything thrown at me that day. There are days too many to count that I have to hold up the white flag and say, "Help, I can't function today"…over the years but I still have the responsibilities of life. I have two dogs now so they have to get let out.

I used to have to walk my dogs two to three times a day, 365. Now I have a yard so I don't have to walk the dogs, but when I can I still do. I have to feed them otherwise no one else does. Then after that, I will just surrender and lay on the couch or my bed and rest for the day to recuperate, sometimes it takes several days. At least now I don't have the added stress from an unsupportive spouse and family. The negative hurtful things I've been told and called over the last 23 years have cut me like a knife, it would have been better to just be hit because I would have left sooner. Now I don't have to worry that anyone will ridicule or call me names or lazy. I still get stressed, my depression is severe, and I wonder if he will tire of me also living this unpredictable crazy life. After living and surviving three years on my own, I know I will be okay. One thing about this damn insidious, evil, heartbreaking *disease*…is if I can *battle* this creature inside me, I can battle and survive anything! *And so can you!*

My Pets Have My Back

By Emily Hinchcliff

My story began in 2010 with being diagnosed with *Chiari I Malformation*, a rare condition that occurs when the brain shifts and settles on top of the spinal cord. It cuts off the cerebral spinal fluid which causes severe headaches and migraines. Therefore, brain surgery is usually used to correct the problem and a shunt is placed to help the fluid continue to flow normally. This was done later that year. Then in 2011 I was diagnosed with Behcet's Disease. This is a rare autoimmune disease that affects the blood vessels in the body. The vessels, when attacked, can burst causing stroke, pulmonary aneurysm, bleeding ulcers, etc. Most common problems result in blindness, mouth sores, genital sores, fatigue. There is no cure. Making sure the immune system is suppressed is very important. But that causes problems also because the body then has trouble fighting off illness. Routine blood work is needed to monitor white and red blood cell counts. These two events help to explain why I believe I was predisposed to the development of *fibromyalgia* later in 2016.

Before my fibro diagnosis, the pain and fatigue I experienced was not a problem. The pain and fatigue became so troublesome by 2016 that they drove me to seek out my doctor, yet again.

Being given a diagnosis and accepting it are two different things.

Once my fibro illness began, my life took an unplanned adventure with my pets who have been my saving grace when dealing with my heath.

I have two cats who I love dearly. They are both males and were both rescued from dire situations. Charlie, *a.k.a. Moo*, was found outside our house and, of course, my daughter insisted on keeping him. He was skinny and covered in fleas. We cleaned him up and brought him in the house as our first beloved and he has remained here since. Charlie is now about 18 lbs and the happiest boy I know. Duncan Tyler was brought to us as a one lb kitty who was abandoned by his mother. My heart broke when I first saw him. His ears were bigger than his body. Charlie took him under his paw and showed him the lay of the house and he has since become my snuggle buddy. Our Duncan is so sensitive. He knows when I don't feel good, he knows when my body hurts, and can even tell when I have trouble breathing because he will put his nose in mine to make sure I am ok. Both kitties have become a constant in my life.

I have two dogs that help round out our loving family. They hold my heart and bring such complete comfort. Pippa, *a boxer/mastiff mix,* weighs in at 100 lbs! She is pure love and has a wiggle butt. Her whole life's mission is to make me smile and watch over me. Her personality is one of a kind. Our other dog, also a girl, is Penelope. *She is a mixed breed* and is 55 lbs of kindness and love, although very protective of her mama! Penelope's favorite past time is also snuggling with me, although I occasionally take a back seat to a bone. Ha Ha!

The emotional and physical trauma I have lived through have taught me to rely on these animals that have given me such joy. Whether I need to talk, hug, or cry with them and have been known to occasionally even scream, they listen. They have never once left my side, or turned their head which I have learned is so different that people can be. They forgive and understand beyond what I can explain. Laying on my lap, as if to say, "Mom. It will be okay, I'll hug you until you are better." They have even kissed my cheek.

The love and support I receive from my pets and return to them is unconditional and very hard to explain. But again, unlike humans, they never look down on me for sleeping all day, or crying all day either, not even for complaining of the pain all day. This nonjudgmental support sustains me and is a gift I will carry with me always.

I only wish that these 'babies' were going to last my lifetime. My pets came into my life for a reason and I am not one to question that. Only God knows the full reason. I do know that if they are here for me, alone, that I want to make sure their lives are as awesome as possible.

Most recently, I have been blessed with a grandbaby. Molly Mae, *a.k.a. Nugget, a miniature dachshund.* She is 10 lbs of fun and joy! She loves her 'grandmother' and will not hesitate to hug and kiss me when she sees me, which is pretty often. Although she lives with my daughter in another town, she FaceTimes me every day just to say Hi!

Such lovely moments are how I distract myself from the pain and fatigue. As you can see my pets are my biggest comfort when it comes to all my health issues. These family members make me forget that I am truly very sick, and for just a little while throughout the day, I can focus on something and someone other than myself.

These animals depend on me to take care of them and that gives me purpose. Each and every day I get up and make the best of what life has thrown at me by caring and loving my 'babies' and I do this with all my heart and soul.

The Game

By Fiona Young

Ricki pushed open the door to Mary's Cafe, scanning the interior quickly.

An oblong box was tucked under her arm. She nodded to a waitress pouring coffee for another customer and made her way across the checkerboard floor to the back. Friendly arms spotted her, waving like friendly flags.

"Ricki!" sang out three voices. The three women who owned the voices swept away the debris from their meal, clearing a space. Ricki placed the box in front of them, grinning.

"Is this it? Is it done?!" The voice belonged to Alex, a 40ish redhead who could barely contain her excitement.

"Almost," answered Ricki, sipping the coffee the waitress had just brought. "A few finishing touches, and your comments needed."

Alex reached for the box but hesitated, looking at the others. "Well, go ahead," growled Connie, a self-avowed Crone in her 60's. Cat, her twin, remained silent, but her eyes shone with excitement. Alex eagerly tore off the brown paper wrapping, casting it aside.

The box contained a Monopoly game. Alex looked aggrieved. Ricki took off the top of the board, nodding to Alex, who took out the board and unfolded it. Every square on the board had been modified with paper squares attached in their place.

"Ladies," declared Ricki, I give you *Fibropoly*! A gamed dedicated to the lucky folks blessed with fibromyalgia. We now have a method of dealing with this mess in a nonviolent, satisfying way."

"I'll be a judge of that," said Connie, pulling the board closer. For a moment, the group seemed to hold its collective breath. Even Ricki, normally talkative, remained quiet. As they waited, a low rumbling sounded at the table. As they waited a bit more, the rumbling grew louder until soon a hearty guffaw rocked the window and eventually unfolded into a tsunami of laughter.

"So, Connie, you like?" grinned Ricki.

Connie was still laughing, unable to speak. She pointed to Cat and Alex.

"All the railroads have been changed to doctor's offices," she laughed.

"And the Electric Company and the Water Company are Social Security Offices," squealed Cat.

By now Connie had herself under control and was busy scrutinizing the board. "Where's Park Place?"

Ricki pointed to a square labeled *Clinique Suisse*. "It's a concierge doctor in Switzerland. You go there, they give you anything you want for the pain. You can have room service or doctor service 24 hours a day, no questions asked. Nobody tells you to lose weight or exercise or that this "so-called illness" is in your head. They put you in a room of doctors and you get to order *them* to the shrink for counseling, and they have to go!"

"Is that a real place?" Alex sighed.

Ricki put her hand on Alex's shoulder, squeezing it lightly. "No, I made it up. But you can win it during the game."

She was rewarded with a collective sigh.

"What else?" asked Connie.

"Well, in the Community Chest we've got Disability Lawyers & Social Worker Services that automatically get in touch with you as soon as you have a diagnosis."

"In the Chance Cards you've got spouses, parents, and others who don't believe you, children who move in with you and demand you do everything for them, and set you back several spaces. Also, there are pharmacies that won't fill your prescriptions, causing you to lose turns. Stuff like that."

Cat opened a small brown bag and emptied the contents. "The game pieces!"

The game pieces consisted of miniatures: a wine cork, the top to a prescription bottle, a tiny blood pressure cuff, an empty vial of vape oil, and a cat.

Alex glanced at the board. "Where's that Income Tax thing?"

Ricki pointed. "It's there. It says 'Your prescriptions have just gone up 40 percent. Proceed to the nearest lawyer's office or give up and just smoke weed.'"

Ricki drained her coffee. "Well?"

"Roll the dice, Ricki, you genius," declared Connie. "Let's play." And so they did.

Through Perseverance, There's Hope

By Penny Weaver Rice

Living with Fibromyalgia has taken a toll on my life. It has changed me in so many ways, from my personal life to my professional life. Every day, I wake in pain so extreme that sometimes my fiancé has to help me out of the bed. I feel so sick and nauseous and get so dizzy I could pass out. When I lie down to sleep I have difficulty breathing and gasp for air in the middle of the night. Doctors say sleep apnea plays a part. It truly scares me! I pray every night that I will wake-up in the morning.

My neurosurgeon says I also have lymphedema of chest glands with swelling in my neck and chest. I thought it was from the titanium that was placed in my neck at C-3 through C-7. My spine is fractured, herniated, and bulging in all three areas of the spine: cervical, thoracic, and lumbar. So far, I have had three spinal surgeries. Even though I continue to move daily to keep my muscles from spasming, the pain is just getting worse. I have extremely bad headaches. Left leg tendons are swelling with a tear in the gastrocnemius muscle, which is causing extreme pain. My left arm has tennis elbow and I have sciatica pain off and on. I am so weak and extremely tired. My immune system is down, so infections are very easy to get. I pray every day to God to continue to heal me because I cannot do this on my own.

Just recently, I became very ill with salmonella poisoning. I had it for 30 plus days. Cypro and Flagyl are continuously given to me by my gastroenterologist. I have also had an endoscopy and colonoscopy where they found polyps and took four biopsies. I'm praying that it's not cancer.

I struggle to keep up with my daily activities of cleaning, cooking and exercise due to weakness, throwing up, nausea, and severe pain. As for my personal life, I continue to try and not to focus on my pain by keeping busy with life and entertaining. Nothing will take it away but distraction helps.

I have no motivation for a sex life. I just don't care about it. I pray this doesn't make my fiancé decide to leave me because he is my strength. He is very supportive, as he has watched his mother suffer through arthritis and fibro.

I continue to work even though I feel sick. I take care of patients that are sick like most of us, so I can relate to them. Recently I had a CAT scan done and was diagnosed with several stomach issues. I have melena, colitis, diverticulitis, GERD, and abdominal masses. I believe the Lord has his mind made up and will continue to help me through this darkness.

My fibro has caused so many issues in my life. The muscle spasms are unbearable. My memory is also getting worse. In the last two years, my eyesight has deteriorating badly. I just feel like my body is dying. *Did I eat something wrong or do something wrong for this to be happening to my body?* I have been given meds to take throughout my life, but I am highly allergic to many pain meds, so I continue to suffer. I was taking Tylenol and ibuprofen but it caused a lot of my abdominal pain, and now I am paying the price. I do eat very healthy. Lots of veggies, fruits, and proteins. There isn't much I don't like but I continue to watch dairy, sugars, carbs, and preservatives. I want to stay away from these things that make my body react negatively. Bread and anything white also hurts me.

Throughout my life, I have had many accidents, changes, and tragedies. I am divorced since 2001 and raised three children on my own with no child support. I have worked three jobs to take care of my family. I worked in law enforcement, nursing as a CNA, and at one point, I owned a cleaning company for ten years, self-employed.

Considering the accidents I have had in my life, I don't know how I am still alive. I have fallen down flights of stairs at least five times and even fallen off a quarter horse, fracturing my hip. I was also in a boating accident where my best friend and I almost lost our lives as we were thrown from the boat. At that moment, I didn't know if we were going to be ok or not. It caused a lot of spinal issues for me and my best friend is very lucky to have survived!

I thank God every day for being alive and being able to walk, talk, and see, for I have seen worse. Some of the people I work for are quadriplegic, can't speak, have autism, can't see, etc. I have also worked with hospice, taking care of people who are dying. Believe me, I have seen it all. I am still thankful for God giving me what I have. I just pray for everyone who has fibro that He gives us all the strength to keep moving, stay healthy and stay safe.

Fibro Men: Interviews

By Doug Kuriger

Fibromyalgia is a predominately woman's illness, but it does not discriminate, men receive this diagnosis too. This chapter contains interviews that fibro men have answered.

INTERVIEW 1

Q) When did you first notice symptoms? At what age?
I have had symptoms since my mid 30's but didn't know what it was. 47.

Q) Can you list your fibro symptoms?
Sensitivity to cold, tender skin, sore joints, exhaustion, sore and tired muscles.

Q) Have you tried different medicines or therapies? Did they work?
Gabapentin, but I'm being weaned off that because the side effects outweigh the treatment.

Q) How would you describe yourself "before fibro" vs. "after your diagnosis"? Are you able to do the same things you could before fibro? Have some things become more difficult?
Everything is a struggle. I am so tired all the time that I just want to sleep. I'm too tired and sore most days to do the things I used to enjoy.

Q) Do you experience depression or anxiety?
Yes, both, but the depression is more crippling than the anxiety.

Q) Any sleep disturbances?

I rarely sleep well. I'm never rested when I am awake.

Q) Do you need a CPAP/other sleep machine?
I have a CPAP machine.

Q) Do you take medication(s) to sleep?
I probably should but I don't want to take sleep aids.

Q) If you could tell doctors anything and knew they would listen, what would it be? (Example, your feeling of whether your doctor(s) show compassion, etc.?)
My doctor listens and seems to empathize but I don't know that she understands. Some of the symptoms are difficult to put into words for someone who hasn't experienced it.

Q) Do you experience other illnesses? Can you put these in a timeline?
I have had chronic pain and migraines since my 20's. I used to be muscular and strong, now I'm weak but I have high muscle tone. I sometimes feel like my muscles and joints are slowly stiffening into rocks. Three years ago, I started getting ocular migraines.

Q) If you could explain fibro "from a man's point of view," what would you say?
I'm a newlywed but have trouble with intimacy. It's difficult to continue for long due to pain and exhaustion.

Q) Is there any advice you could give that would help other men deal with fibro better?
Ask for help, there are people out there that understand! I know it's hard to do but you don't have to live half a life!

Q) What are the top three things about fibro that concern you the most? For example, I would say (1) loss of independence, (2) needing to ask for help, (3) lack of knowledgeable medical help.
1) Loss of independence, 2) Lack of medical care, 3) Needing to ask for help. These are my top three too. I have always been someone

that did everything myself, so it's very difficult to have someone else tie my shoes or carry things for me. It's hard to find the right medical treatments. It seems like the doctors are at as much of a loss as we are and just throw medicine at the symptoms, hoping one of them will do the trick.

INTERVIEW 2

Q) When did you first notice symptoms? At what age?
Probably when my pain started in my mid 30's. I am now 42.

Q) Can you list your fibro symptoms?
Pain that will not go away, no matter what.

Q) Have you tried different medicines or therapies? Did they work?
Yes, I have tried multiple medications even a natural one. None had worked until I got on Lyrica. I also feel aqua therapy helps.

Q) How would you describe yourself "before fibro" vs. "after your diagnosis"? Are you able to do the same things you could before fibro? Have some things become more difficult?
I could walk for hours and miles and could drive for hours without issues before my dx. After, I have to pace myself. I need to take my time doing anything, even baking! I can only do the activity for so long. It also takes me longer to do most of the things I use to.

Q) Do you experience depression or anxiety?
Yes. I have been diagnosed with severe depression.

Q) Any sleep disturbances?
Yes. I have trouble at times, but not often.

Q) Do you need a CPAP/other sleep machine?
No.

Q) Do you take medication(s) to sleep?

Yes.

Q) If you could tell doctors anything, and knew they would listen, what would it be? (Example, your feeling of whether your doctor(s) show compassion, etc.?)
My old doctor gave up on me. I would like to say to her, "I wish you could live a day in my shoes so you know what I go through." My current doctor, however, listens to me and what I say. I am believed and I want to say thank you!

Q) Do you experience other illnesses? Can you put these in a timeline?
Yes. No, I really do not remember in what order. I just felt like I started falling apart.

Q) If you could explain fibro "from a man's point of view," what would you say?
Omg, yes! If you can take the worst pain you can think of and triple it—then think of that pain and how it will never end. It is always constant.

Q) Is there any advice you could give that would help other men deal with fibro better?
Talk to your doctor honestly. Do not be afraid to talk to people about it as well. I do wish there were support groups for just us guys.

Q) What are the top three things about fibro that concern you the most? For example, I would say (1) loss of independence, (2) needing to ask for help, (3) lack of knowledgeable medical help.
1) Memory issues would be first. 2) Loss of independence. 3) Having to ask for help would be next. 4) Not being able to do things by myself any longer. (Simple things like opening a soda bottle.)

INTERVIEW 3

Q) When did you first notice symptoms? At what age?

I probably started noticing my symptoms when I was nine or ten. I was officially diagnosed with amplified pain syndrome at the age of 12. The doctors refused to give me the true diagnosis of fibromyalgia, because they didn't want to burden me with a label. I will be 16 on February 28.

Q) Can you list your fibro symptoms?
Body pain throughout, especially in my back. I don't have the stamina to sit in a classroom all day. At times, my legs feel like lead weights.

Q) Have you tried different medicines or therapies? Did they work?
I have tried massage therapy and biofeedback therapy. I see a CBT (cognitive behavioral therapist) at Children's Mercy Hospital in KCMO. I regularly see the doctor in the pain management clinic. The doctors refuse to prescribe me any pain medication. I have to get by with over-the-counter medicine.
I do get relief with the family chiropractor, but it's not covered by insurance.
I also have a TENS unit that I can use all over my body.
I use Bio-freeze, but it only helps a little.
When I suffer a migraine that lasts more than three days, I go in for a peri-cranial nerve block. (These I have gotten multiple times.)

Q) How would you describe yourself "before fibro" vs. "after your diagnosis"? Are you able to do the same things you could before fibro? Have some things become more difficult?
I really can't remember a time before fibromyalgia took over my body. My little sister does all the things that I wish I could do. She plays football for her school. She also wrestles and can ride her bike for miles. I feel like I have to live vicariously through her.

Q) Do you experience depression or anxiety?
Yes, both.

Q) Any sleep disturbances?
After a seizure I'm especially fatigued. I can sleep when I need to.

Q) Do you need a CPAP/other sleep machine?
No.

Q) Do you take medication(s) to sleep?
No.

Q) If you could tell doctors anything, and knew they would listen, what would it be? (Example, your feeling of whether your doctor(s) show compassion, etc.?)
I think my doctors have listened to me.

Q) Do you experience other illnesses? Can you put these in a timeline?
I have also been diagnosed with a number of other things. These include autism, ADHD, anxiety, bipolar mood disorder, depression, asthma, eczema, sensory processing disorder, EOE, ulcers, migraine headaches, and psychogenic seizures.
I do not have a timeline. All of this has always just been here.
When I am in a big "flare," I will go into a psychogenic seizure. While my brain is not at risk, I suffer all the other symptoms of someone having a "real" seizure. My body shakes anywhere from two minutes to two hours. I have no recollection of the event. My head hurts and I'm exhausted. (These seizures are the number one reason why I am unable to attend a traditional high school. My pain would shoot to a 9/10. This, in turn, would raise my anxiety levels, and trigger a seizure. A vicious cycle.)

Q) If you could explain fibro "from a man's point of view," what would you say?
I really don't know how my experiences differ from that of a woman.

Q) Is there any advice you could give that would help other boys/young men deal with fibro better?
I would tell them that they are not alone. Don't let others *BULLY* you because you are sick. Don't back down. Fight to get the right diagnosis.

My mom has never given up on me. She's always been supportive. We've traveled hundreds of miles in order to be heard. She even fought for me to get SSI. That's huge! I won't have to worry about not being able to hold down a full time job.

Q) What are the top three things about fibro that concern you the most? For example, I would say (1) loss of independence, (2) needing to ask for help, (3) lack of knowledgeable medical help.
The top three things that concern me are (1) Why me? What did I do as a child to get this? (2) Why do so many people not believe in fibromyalgia? (3) When will there be a cure/helpful treatment?

Comparing symptoms and similar questions I must conclude gender does *NOT* interfere with the various symptoms seen in fibromyalgia. Each person has a combination of such individual symptoms, both men and women. Due to the way men and women react differently to the same symptoms and approach their problems with different thought patterns, I have to conclude that gender is not a defining item. Looking into predisposition (genetics) or "environmental factors" may be the only identical items we can study further. These include being exposed to the same stimuli—genetics, environmental toxins, chemicals, allergies, stress and/or trauma.

My Fibro Story, So Far...

By Sharonda, *UK*

I am a married 45-year-old mum and I have three children, a 24-year-old, 21-year-old, and a five-year-old. I started on my fibromyalgia journey a year and a half ago thinking that I had a brain tumor! I had many terrible pains in the right side of my head. Imagine someone squeezing your arm so tightly that it hurts, then imagine that going into your head. It got to the point where I was crying with the pain and my husband kept saying I needed to see the doctor. As always it was hard to get an appointment and my husband insisted on taking me to the A/E at our hospital after a particularly bad episode.

They did their checks and said they didn't think it was a brain tumor but that I needed to get into my doctors and ask for an MRI. I eventually saw my doctor who referred me for one. At my *first* MRI, I was laid down and fastened in and we were ready to go. Unfortunately, my claustrophobia kicked in and they said they have never seen someone get out of everything and off the table so fast! *Not a good start.* The clinician said that for my next MRI I would probably need a sedative. Off I went to the doctors again, explained what had happened and got my next referral for my MRI and now had my sedative prescription, *all good I thought.* Took my sedative and was pretty chilled on the way to the hospital. We got there and found out it was the day before! *Second failed attempt.* For my third MRI, I took my sedatives and just kept saying to myself I have to do this, I have to do this. I had to have someone with me in the room holding my hand, have an eye mask on and earplugs in, but I was proud that I finally did it. *Yay!*

Off I went to the doctor for the results. I was told that I have three or four bad vertebrae in my upper neck and that I have degenerative disc disease. I was asked if I would try acupuncture of which

I said yes as I really wanted to get rid of my constant pain. I had three or four sessions of this with my physiotherapist and we both agreed that it was not working. At this stage, I was waking up in the mornings crying with neck and shoulder pain. I asked the lady if it could be fibro, of which she said she was starting to think along those lines. Again, I went back to my doctor and she referred me to a rheumatologist because of our concerns about fibro. In the meantime, I was prescribed Zapain and Amitriptyline to help with my pain. The rheumatologist after our chat asked me to lay down. He started pressing points on my body, these were what I now know as "trigger points." Well as he got to my inner knees, the pain nearly sent me flying off the table! I would have happily hit him at this point. He said he wouldn't do any more points as he could tell I was in a lot of pain. When feeling my knees, the rheumatologist said that I also had osteoarthritis and at some point would need an operation on my knees. *Great!* We sat down after and he asked me for some background information. Did I ever have a bad car accident? Yes—many years ago where I was thrown two feet across the car and had severe whiplash and the car was 'totaled.' Did any of my family have fibro? *Yes—my mum, two aunts, and my grandma.* Apparently, the more members you have in your family with fibro the higher your chances of getting it, as it can be inherited. *Great!* In his opinion I have fibro. I was asked if I would try Hydrotherapy. I said yes anything to try and alleviate my pain. Again, I had to go back to my doctor to discuss. Initially, I was put on Naproxen as well as other tablets because of the amount of pain I was in but cautioned to only take with *bad* episodes. This is because it's classified as a good tablet but can cause internal problems.

My appointment came through for my hydrotherapy which sounded good. *The first week after the class was absolute torture.* Obviously, you use different muscles but because it's done in water it's supposed to be better. I didn't find this to be the case but still went ahead with the next week's session and the following weeks ahead. As my sessions ended the therapist asked if it had helped me at all—of which I said no, not at all, and she said that many had said that is the case. I guess it works for some but not for others. So back to the doctor I went.

I must say that the doctor I see for my fibro was *very* supportive, which I am very fortunate with. I have read other peoples stories where this isn't the case, and these people have my sympathy. We discussed everything and also my tablets. Currently I am on Zapain, Duloxetine, Amitriptyline, Fexofenadine (for allergies), turmeric capsules, peppermint capsules for my IBS and a few other natural remedies, daily. Of my Amitriptyline tablets, my doctor recommended upping my dose from 30mg to 50mg to knock the edge more off my pain. Well... I tried this, only to find myself getting very depressed and upset more easily. The higher dose made me feel like I was in a zombie state. My husband said I needed to go back to the doctors again. Off I went. My doctor suggested dropping back down which I feel better about. I asked my doctor if there was anything else that I could try. She said that pain relief for fibro is basically rubbish, but if I did hear of anything to let her know so that we can explore. I was told at the hospital that it takes one to two years for a person with fibro to get their head around having the condition! *One to two years!* When I was told this, I burst into tears. I felt like my old life had ended and here I am being in constant pain. I just didn't know how I would cope.

My pre-fibro life was good. I could keep the house tidy, look after my husband and daughter with no aided help *and* do extra jobs either in the house or garden and feel okay. Now I am just a shadow of the former person I was, which my husband has commented on. I wake up more times than not in pain, and my husband gets my tablets out for me and has them ready in a morning. It takes at least an hour for these to start kicking in before I can start properly moving. By this time, our five-year-old must be up and getting ready for school. If I don't get this timed out before, it stresses me which in turn affects my fibro. On a good day, I still hurt all over but I can move. On a bad day, I feel like an old woman. I walk slowly and the pain gets bad...even with tablets. On these days, my husband (who usually works from home) has to help our daughter get ready and run her to school. These days I literally can do nothing and I mean *nothing.* My husband has to do everything for me, including scratch my back if I have an itch, undo my bra, etc.

These have to be sleep days that include even more sleep. Sleeping all day does not provide proper restful sleep, however. I have to give my husband a lot of credit since I've been diagnosed with fibro. Even before fibro he was helpful but he has really stepped up since my diagnosis. He tells me not to stress about the things I now cannot do and does them for me. He does the dishwasher, tidies the downstairs, cooks and looks after me making sure I get my tablets, eat, etc. He says he can tell from my face when I'm in tremendous pain and probably because I walk like an 80 year old around the house at my worst.

To be honest, I am an easily stressed person anyway but fibro compounds it even more. I'm still at the stage of trying to get my head around having this terrible disease and do try not to let things stress me out any further. I am house proud, so all this not doing or not even having the energy to do things is still new to me. If I do have a semi-good day, I try to do like most others, and catch up on things. *Whoa it's to my detriment!* I pay for it the next few days. Sometimes I try to sneak an energy drink in so that I can feel a bit better, but my husband tells me off and says they're not good for me (to be honest he's right and it doesn't help my flares). Just sometimes I need to feel sort of normal and block fibro from my head but I know my husband is right. I get night sweats, out of breath, I talk rubbish sometimes—worse than normally, and get my words mixed up and the fibro fog is terrible. I've also found that I have put some weight on with my Amitriptyline tablets. *That's another discussion for the doctor. I'm so fed up with going to the doctor that when I need to go I put it off? That's where I am at the moment.*

With fibro fog...it now takes me twice as long to make dinner! I can plan the meal but while cooking I forget what I'm doing and stand at the fridge looking, trying to remember what I went in there for. It is a running joke now with my friends when they come around for dinner about how long it takes me to cook. My husband has to check once I've finished that I've turned the oven off because I have left the stove on all night at times. When we lock the house up, before going to bed, he has to go round after me because two nights in a row I have left the downstairs windows open all night. For me, that is a definite no-no because I am very safety conscious due to getting robbed on two occasions. I was sure I had shut all the windows but apparently not.

The fibro fog is just as bad with driving. I used to be a very confident driver and have driven for many years and would travel to just about anywhere. Now, I'm not. I find it hard to concentrate at times. It's hard to describe, it's as if I get a scared feeling. I grip that steering wheel so tight and have to really focus and countdown to getting home. I probably can drive up to about 25 miles now and even then it's too much. Before fibro I could drive forever. All the things listed above are so frustrating and all because of fibro. I keep having to repeat things I say as I get the words wrong or just simply cannot describe what I want. It becomes a game of charades sometimes when I'm trying to explain something.

And the breathlessness! If I do anything my heart rate shoots up and I get pains in my chest. *Another part of fibro I am told.* One thing I've found that definitely helps my fibro is going for a body massage once a month. The beautician knows what techniques to use for a fibro client. Yes, it hurts that day and for a couple of days after, but then I find I am more mobile which I'm grateful for. When my appointment time for the next one comes around it's as if my body knows and is ready for it. I've tried reflexology but that didn't work for me. I'm open to trying anything that will improve my quality of life but until then, it's just a case of finding what works for me.

I've also learned how to deal with hip and knee pain. They have become everyday normal things to me. I feel at times that I'm trapped in another person's body screaming to get out and let the old me back. Obviously, I get down with it all, I'm sure each and every person that has fibro does. I would never have thought that an illness like this would have so many different things going hand in hand with it. For those that don't have fibro, we probably look normal on the outside because all our ailments are on the inside. To those people, I wouldn't wish fibro on anyone but would like them to have one day in our bodies to feel how painful and debilitating this illness can be.

Knowing fibro can be inherited worries me because I wouldn't wish this on either of my daughters! My eldest daughter is developing some similar symptoms at 21 and I hope the future will bring a treatment for fibro. *I have quite a high tolerance for pain but fibro pain is brutal!* I am in pain an estimated 95 percent of the time. Tablets help but do not take the pain away completely, so it's learning to deal with and find ways to cope that works for me. I've been in a flare up all week. When I am in a very bad flare, I cannot do *anything*, which is upsetting. The pain just makes you not want to do anything...even going to the toilet is hard.

On these days my husband has to do everything and I mean everything! In a roundabout way my fibro story is still ongoing and always will be. There is no cure for it I'm told. So, if you suspect that you have fibro and for those of you, like me, that are on the long fibro path...you have to find something that works for you. It's a very nasty disease that robs you and your life of so much. It needs to be brought to the forefront for everyone so more can be done for this disease. It is up to us as fibro warriors to make others aware of this condition and help each other on our fibro path together. Even now I realize that I haven't remembered to write down everything I wanted to. Please, if you think you have fibro go to the doctor and find ways to manage it so it doesn't ruin your life. Know there is a community of us willing to walk the journey with you!

Dear Diary,

Well, today is Saturday. The weekends I class as "proper" family time and what am I doing? I'm lying on the sofa with my warming pad (of which my husband says I look like a nun! Cheeky!) around my neck and shoulders trying to cope with the pain that I have all over. I got out of bed feeling like an 80 year-old woman. I slowly made my way downstairs as the pains in my ankles and feet were hurting, and every step made me wince in pain with my knees and hips. I take all the tablets that my husband got out for me and I'm waiting for them to kick in so that I can get some relief. Today I hurt so much everywhere. I hate these days and they get me down. After my morning drink, I have to lie down because I am not getting any help from the pain. So I lay here, watching my husband look after me and our daughter. My husband, bless him, says he can see the pain in my eyes. All I can say is that it's like having a really bad dose of the flu except it doesn't go away, you just get different levels of it. On these down days, it's like the old me cries silently inside. I used to be so able to do anything and everything. Now I'm just a shell of that former person. *I ask myself why do I have to deal with fibro? Why can't it be someone else?* I'm not a horrible person and I would say that I had a pretty much perfect life before this. I have a nice home with someone that loves me for who I am, quirks and all. I see my children and they're happy. *What do I give them?* A person that I feel is a burden to everyone, whereas before, it was me that looked after everyone. Laying on the sofa gives you a lot of time to think! Even now I'm getting a little emotional writing this down as I remember things. Never mind that my family says that I am different, what about me?! I see that I'm different and I feel an inner sadness for what I have lost, and for everyone around me. I don't mean to sound selfish, but there is a buildup of anger inside of me because I just can't get used to this other person. I feel like getting out of this body and giving it a good shake to bring "me" back. My pains still aren't getting better yet, even with my warming pad on high. I would say my pain level today is an 11. It's a really bad day. My pain level tolerance is quite high, but on these days I struggle to hang on. It's like all the insides of me hurt. I even put off going to the bathroom because of having to move and be in even more pain. A normal pain day for me is a seven or eight. I am in continuous pain all day every day, it just has differing levels of intensity. Today the pain is making me feel sick and giving me a headache. When I'm in pain just lying down like this is when I hate fibro the most. I imagine running to the edge of a cliff and just screaming.

Before 'fibro', I was thinking about taking a college course or once our daughter started primary school. I thought that I would better myself somehow once I had more time. *Well that has gone out the window! Another reason to hate fibro!* I do think of people who have fibro and work and I take my hat off to them because I couldn't do it. I have found out there are varying levels in fibro. I also think there needs to be something on the market soon to help treat fibro. I...need something better because I just can't go through years like this. They say this is a chronic pain condition...well they weren't wrong with that one! But hey, tomorrow is another day and I refuse to let 'this' beat me! I'm not one of those people that gives in or gives up. So after my lunch that my husband has just brought in, I'm off for an Epsom bath and to chill, both seem to help. Then next week I will start my regime of walking again each day. That seem to help too, even though I don't want to go at times. Then next week I've got my massage and facial to look forward to. Hopefully tomorrow I can do a bit of tidying up the mess around me, but hey, as I said... tomorrow *is* another day!

My Daughter's Journey

By *A Canadian Advocate*

This chapter is different from the other chapters. In this chapter, a mother and daughter write their experiences and fears as they watch "like mother, like daughter" become a reality. The daughter develops fibromyalgia! This is an extremely difficult experience, so the daughter asked not to be named.

I am writing this chapter as worry fills my heart, one of my biggest fears seem to be surfacing. My 18-year-old daughter is showing signs and symptoms of fibromyalgia. I am hoping that my fears will help motivate all medical professionals to find a cure. The cure is not just for those who already suffer this horrible pain but it is to protect our children from the same pain.

I was diagnosed two years ago and realized that I was *not* going crazy. My pain is real and it is called fibromyalgia. I now look back over my daughter's life and see her symptoms actually started when she was a child. *This puts the fear of God in me!* By eight, she had already had three ear surgeries due to many excruciatingly ear infections. I remember many nights of her screaming in pain with high fevers. We ran out of options for antibiotics because they stopped working for her. I had suffered from painful ear infections as a child also. She continues to get painful headaches, sinus infections and constant nose bleeds. I also still suffer from sinus infections, headaches, and when young nose bleeds. It's surreal to think I would say, "Honey, I suffered from all of these as a child too. You must take after me." Oh my God, I wish I could take back those words! I cannot describe the worrying I have, that she does take after me.

When she hit puberty and started her period everything was fine for the first few years. Then she started having horrible period cramps. I had horrible cramps at her age and again I thought she took after me. Later in life, I had to have a hysterectomy because I had adenomyosis. I pray every day that she does not have this as well! When she was a child and even into her teens she suffered from growing pains, screaming through the night. Sharp pains coming from out of nowhere. I also had those growing pains.

She now complains of morning stiffness and how long it takes her to get moving in the morning. I suffer from morning stiffness. The random burning sensations or the feeling of ice cubes running down your legs, we share those symptoms too. We also have anxiety, knee pain, joint pain, and upper back pain in common.

When I was a young teen, I used to complain to my doctor about my upper back pain and my doctor would ask if I didn't mean lower back pain. She has so much pain in her neck and hands. She complained about hand pain when she was just a little girl! When she was growing up I had no idea what fibro was or that it even existed. She complains to me that she cannot keep her cell phone in her back pocket because it hurts her hip. *Can you imagine that a thing as light as a phone can cause her hip pain?* She complains about the pain in her toe. I had to have a Marin Fusion on my right toe. The thought of her ever having to have this surgery completely destroys me. I never want her to have to go through that type of intense pain!

I need to explain that my daughter didn't know I suffered from fibro as she grew, because I didn't even know. It breaks my heart to realize that we suffered from the same symptoms growing up. My daughter had no idea what fibro was or what its symptoms were until I was diagnosed. Now she may get the same diagnosis? I am grateful that because I suffer, I can give her the moral and mental support that she needs. I will advocate for her. I will make sure she receives the right medical care from the same wonderful and amazing medical professionals that I have. Most importantly she will know that I do not think she is crazy! She will know what she is experiencing is real and not something made up in her head. I will not allow her to be made to feel the way I was, dismissed to the point that I thought I was going crazy! She has my support and the support of her family and friends who see what I've gone through. I am able to share all of the tips and tricks that are in this book that were provided by all of the contributors. I can teach her how to pace herself to help her complete her tasks and feel good about herself. I am grateful that at the moment she is able to double major in university and stay focused on her studies. Sometimes the anxiety proves to be too much for her but our family helps her get through it. She was just recognized for her academic achievements. She's in the top 15 percent of her program and made the Golden Key High Society! I want my daughter to be able to physically/mentally become; the Broadway star, the clinical psychologist, the teacher, or whatever she wants to be. I want her to *NOT* suffer from brain fog, anxiety, depression, insomnia, or widespread pain as we all do.

My daughter having to take all the necessary meds that I take kills me. I have tried to go without them and I simply cannot without giving up my quality of life. It takes my breath away to think this may be her future too. We need a cure to stop this vicious circle of suffering! My daughter and I suffer from fibro and two other family members suffer from RA. I know that we cannot stop our genes from being passed down but if we could simply find a cure, all will be saved! I plead with the medical professionals to not give up! I plead for them to work together from around the world in finding a cure for us all. In the meantime, it's wonderful our children have our support and understanding because we "get it"! *GOD BLESS OUR CHILDREN!*

"There's Toxins In My Meds?"

By Barbara Lyn

After seeing the high amount of book contributors and people in the Fibromyalgia Support Group (as well as the support groups for MS and Breast Cancer I'm in), all ask the same question over and over: "Do any of you suffer from constant itching and hives?" *Another common question is,* "Do many of you have frequent headaches or migraines?"

I knew I needed to write a chapter on these issues. I have found an answer that has surprised me and been confirmed by an allergist. Another doctor who knows of my allergy to various ingredients keeps asking if she can give my name to some of her other patients. They, too, complain of these same symptoms and feel overwhelmed when the allergist confirms that they are also allergic to these pervasive ingredients. PEG and/or PPG, as well as other lesser known chemicals, have become all too familiar to me and others I know.

PEG is the abbreviation for polyethylene glycol, and PPG is the abbreviation for polypropylene glycol. These two chemicals are sisters. It's easy to feel overwhelmed upon learning that you are showing signs of being allergic to these ingredients! I did. PEG alone is in 9000+ products.

You use many of these products daily and often frequently throughout the day. For example; shampoo, cream rinse, soap, hand sanitizer, laundry detergents, dryer sheets, cleaning products, perfume, makeup, medicine, and vitamins. Even eye drops and prenatal vitamins! I think you get the picture. We consume these ingredients often throughout the day and with them accumulating in our bodies they become toxic, pro-ducing an allergy. *Then our livers become overtaxed which causes our body's support system to break down.*

Do I believe that PEG and PPG are part of the toxins/chemicals that over time contribute to the development of fibro, absolutely! This gradual attack on anyone's immune system could cause the multitude of symptoms that manifests in different ways—one being fibromyalgia.

That's quite an introduction to a chapter. I understand that many people who are affected are very much like the doctors who we want to help us, but are so overwhelmed, it's easier to ignore the issue. Unfortunately, at some point you *will* need to address this problem or your symptoms will get worse.

That is what happened to me. I got headaches first but did not recognize that as an allergic symptom or reaction, so I kept using the items that caused it. At that time, the 'extra amount' of PEG was caused by a multivitamin, in combination with my daily life-style. The headaches progressed to visual migraines, but still I didn't relate that to anything. I did mention it to my father-in-law once and he said he got the same reaction with that multivitamin. I thought, hum, that's strange. Then I stopped taking that vitamin and decided to take individual vitamins. Interesting, not so many migraines. Maybe there was a correlation, or maybe it was just a fluke. When I had oxycodone, after a tubal, I had the same problem. Odd. Well, I wasn't going to have that medication again, so I didn't worry about it.

These occurrences happened until a migraine developed and as the migraine diminished I would develop hives during the night. When you have the illnesses I have, fibromyalgia, multiple sclerosis, and recently breast cancer, the last thing you want to deal with is complications! For the next couple of years, I watched what I ate, where I had been, what I had been exposed to. I juggled my illnesses, family life and activities with the sheer grit and determination you find most fibro warriors have. In fact, I can almost predict how many of your friends, family members, co-workers or acquaintances have fibro and other diseases because they are such good actors. I admit, I'm a good actor too. I don't perform on stage but I do put on my makeup and "face" including the smile and lighthearted spirit to fool even the most perceptive people I know. Often times pulling off this masquerade results in hearing the praise of "You look so good!" I even had a very good friend tell me "You must have gotten over your fibro and MS!" Okay, let's be realistic for a moment. You don't 'get over' either of these two illnesses. They are lifelong, chronic diseases that deteriorate a normal active and healthy lifestyle. We all want people to enjoy our company, activities we attend, etc., so we *fake* being *well*. It's true! I'm sorry but you need to know these lies, because each time we "fake it" our health declines more. (Back to trying to enjoy my life or pretend to so my family can enjoy theirs. When you see a person smiling it's easier to have fun around them and that's our goal. If we can't enjoy the activities, we *want* our friends and family to! With 24/7 pain, exhaustion, and a multitude of symptoms, like insomnia, who wouldn't want to pretend?)

Then one weekend the fun activities caught up with me. It wasn't enough to fake happiness because I began getting serious allergic reactions. No more looking good unless I kept my surroundings free from unnecessary items. After attending my husband's company Christmas Gala, I broke out with hives all over! I knew I was allergic to shellfish, so I had stayed away from the sushi bar. My reaction was *so* extreme and I had not eaten or touched *any* seafood. (This became a weekend long event.) My head itched and my skin and the tightness in my throat got bad so I took a Benadryl. Not a smart move. The Benadryl helped my breathing, but as it has PEG in it, it took days for my itching and hives to clear up. Wow. I must have had indirect contact with seafood that evening. Whatever the incident was, it was enough to cause all this itching! I hoped it wouldn't happen again! It *did*. The next time it was worse. It was my PAIN MEDICINE! I had been on the stuff for years. I thought there could be no way my medicine was causing the problem. (You expect some side effects, but they don't continue and become life threatening, do they?)

There was only one way to find out. *I was on a mission!* Armed with a highlighter and time, I started with my meds, looked up all the active and inactive ingredients. I highlighted everything my meds had in common. Then I moved to vitamins, Tylenol, and other supplements. Wow, there seems to be a trend here but nothing concrete. Then I thought, I've always been sensitive to dust, I'll look into my dusting supplies, then, on to my cleaning supplies. By now I *know* I'm on to something. By late afternoon I have gone through everything I touch and use in the house. Only two ingredients in most, only one in all. *PEG*. I had to know for sure, so with just minutes left before 5:00 p.m., I called the allergy department at my medical clinic. I explained that I've been having severe allergic reactions to something and I think I know what it is. Is there a doctor that could see me the next day, and then I started praying. They answered yes; Dr. Moore will see you tomorrow! Yay! During my visit the next day, the doctor was skeptical, but said it was possible that I was right. He did some outside allergy testing, then told me to come back in a week and make sure I had not taken anything or been around any of the irritants until then. I was so thankful that he fit me in so fast. I was impressed that he was concerned enough to sense the urgency of my situation.

The next week I returned, he had a sample of pure PEG from a specialty pharmacy. He did a reactive test, said I wasn't overreactive, so I could be tested that day. He tested me for PEG and I had to wait 15 minutes for the full results. It felt like an hour. You are not allowed to itch, so by the time he came back, I was ready to yank my arm off. He was amazed at the extreme reaction I had. My whole arm was starting to swell. Confirmation clear, I began the daunting test of learning how to live without PEG products.

No Tylenol or Benadryl. (I'm already allergic to Aspirin and Advil.) Once you start reading labels, it's surprising how many things that are labeled organic or green that are clearly not. It's *very hard* to find PEG free items and the pharmacy is the place I have to worry about the most. If drug manufacturers are switched, pharmacists have to catch any change in my meds, or reformulation that includes adding PEG. If companies are bought out, the new meds vary sometimes, and it is *always* the inactive ingredients that contain the problems. PEG is used as a stabilizer and a binder so there is a good reason for it, but gelatin is used in the generic items I can use. Why aren't all medicines, vitamins, and home products using gelatin? Drumroll please, *MONEY.* (It probably costs a cent or two more than PEG.)

The scary part of PEG are the other common uses it has. It is used in cars and refinishing furniture! Well, I can honestly say I don't want it in my body or my family's bodies either! The fact that it is in prenatal vitamins is downright *sick.* Our kids are exposed to these chemicals <u>before</u> they are even born. Don't get me wrong, there are lists of chemicals that are poisoning many consumable products, but these particular two are ranked very high on the toxin list. More and more people are becoming allergic because we use products containing these for everything.

Did you know that if you are waiting for a liver transplant, your worst symptoms—which become increasingly harder to manage—are itching and hives. This can't be a coincidence since the liver is what processes the PEG through your body. The worst part? All of these medicines, vitamins, and products are FDA approved! Crazy! I am sorry to be the bearer of bad news but before more of us become allergic let's bring awareness to not just fibro, but the toxins we consume. Our environment is not helping our illness. PEG and PPG can be taken internally or topically, it also can be inhaled. This is alarming!

This revelation needs to be shared, before we poison ourselves further! That is why I'm writing this chapter, in the middle of the night, while I should be sleeping. With MS, fibromyalgia, breast cancer, the *last thing* I should have to worry about is if the medicine or supplements I'm taking are going to poison me. (Post cancer meds that people are told to take for five to ten years after cancer is treated, consist of five choices. The first has been used the longest, but brings a risk of 50 percent higher chance of stroke. This no. 1 drug concerns me because my family members, while all living long lives—when they have passed—it's due to a stroke. So no. 1 is off the table. The next four are not an option because they *all* contain PEG. Tricky! I can *risk cancer reoccurring* or *take meds with PEG and suffers life threatening breathing trouble.* Not much of an option for me, is it?)

Let's advocate for fibro *and* be smart by also advocating for more *HEALTHY* and *PURE* medicines. These healthy alternatives should *not* cost more just because they are not toxic. They should cost *less*. We need the government to think of our kids, our parents, and our siblings. We need healthy choices so we can become healthier people! Thank you for reading this chapter with an open mind.

Merely Existing

By Lynn Declan

Today Tuesday, July 31, 2018, 1:44 AM, I want to share my journey with Fibromyalgia.

Please be patient while reading the details of my life. I truly believe they will help you understand and possibly prevent your predisposition for developing this illness. If you already have been diagnosed with Fibromyalgia, you may find some healing or comfort in sharing some of my pain. I am sure many of you are wondering why I included so many details of my past below. For me, all the early abuses, stresses, and unending rollercoaster ride of emotions finally took its toll on my body. I believe there are some common denominators in all fibro stories even though we are individuals and handle stress differently.

This is my story and how I feel mental, emotional, physical, and sexual abuse combined with huge amounts of stress and dysfunctional family dynamics took their toll on further damaging my life.

I survived by trying to be a perfectionist and caretaker for everyone else. *Add the toxins I was exposed to and you have a perfect recipe for illness.* I feel that my daughter has the initial symptoms of fibro. This is of great concern to me. Anything I can do to help others understand this debilitating, chronic, painful illness drives me to share my story.

My father was an alcoholic and mom coped the best she could raising four children in a dysfunctional family. I think she merely existed, but her mother/siblings did live in the same community providing support for her. I believe she did not realize the extent of my abuse because of her own problems.

Sexual abuse happened to me around four years of age by an uncle. A few years later, a neighbor boy, and an older brother to a playmate of mine sexually abused us both and threatened us to never say anything.

An old bar buddy of my dad's offered me a ride to my grandmother's house but I ended up never reaching her house and several hours later he dropped me off where he picked me up. I think you can imagine what happened during that time.

In pre-and teenage years the fathers of the children I babysat began sexually abusing me and again threats followed.

I was raped in my late teens several times by acquaintances of the family. Back then I couldn't figure out how this could keep happening to me. During this abuse I suffered from a lot of headaches, lack of energy, no self-esteem, depression, loneliness, and isolation. I was diagnosed with TMJ and the dentist gave me a mouth brace to wear. He also ground down my teeth to stop the night grinding. The neck and jaw pain was so bad I could not participate in PE classes. I was then sent to ENT doctors and finally an endocrinologist. This doctor gave me iodine pills and did a thyroid scan. Apparently, everything checked out ok and the endocrinologist told my mom I was "faking" or "imagining my pain." That was depressing to hear and made me feel like I was crazy.

I could not participate in any school activities and always had to come straight home from school. No friends were ever allowed to my home due to my father's drinking. I struggled but somehow managed to get through high school. About a month before graduation, I found out some of my transcripts never got sent to the nursing school l had applied to. My formal application and class acceptance was put off for another year. This was devastating. I panicked knowing I would not be able to get away from my abusers. Two weeks before graduation, I attempted suicide by overdosing. I received minimal and insincere counseling. After discharge, I refused to continue with counseling as an outpatient. That was when my oldest sister told me I was the reason my mom was on medication for her nerves. She never questioned *if I was okay* though. Guilt, fear, and confusion overcame me.

What was wrong with me? I kept blocking and pushing the pain deep down, inside of myself. It stayed buried for almost 30 years.

I did get into nursing school and graduated. I became a super achiever, wonderful caretaker and a perfectionist as well as kept myself busy with many creative and artistic projects to escape. I dove into my work and was able to vent through my artistic talents. It was there I finally found the acknowledgement and compliments I was lacking from my childhood. I just wanted to be hugged, loved, and accepted for me. After graduating from nursing school my older sister and I took a ten-day vacation tour to Hawaii. I met a very polite, charming local man while there. He promised to come visit me and we corresponded with occasional phone calls. He came to visit, twice. On that second visit, just four months after meeting, he brought along an engagement ring and proposed. People told me it was like a fairytale, but I would later find out I was not like Cinderella. At the same time, all my friends were moving on with their lives and the fear of not being able to make it alone made me panic. I was scared, insecure, and lacked confidence in myself. So I was relieved to be getting married. I would have someone to care for and love me. Six months later we married and I moved to Hawaii, finally away from my abusers.

Vacationing in Hawaii and living as a local is entirely different. Life there was a learning experience for this naive Wisconsin girl. If I felt alone before, I was even more isolated then. I felt like I was dropped off in the middle of the ocean, literally. My father-in-law was very accepting of me but my mother-in-law made it no secret that she did not like me because I was not a local girl. We lived with them for four months and I tried to stay out of her way. I spent a lot of time alone in our small room. I learned (pigeon) English, some Japanese, and took Filipino classes so I would fit in. I was the only "haole" working in the clinic where my job was located. The high cost of living in Hawaii gradually just became part of the reality of living in paradise. We could not afford a trip to visit my family back in Wisconsin for two and a half years because my husband was flat broke. He hid and lied and carried on the deception and huge amount of bills, only confessing once I started watching the mail. On top of that, he blamed me as if the bills were my fault. His two trips to Wisconsin plus a $600 phone bill to call me were just the beginning of the bills. Of course, this was my fault! I also found he had hidden several maxed out charge cards.

I was so in love with him that the dysfunction I experienced growing up made this seem "normal." In my fantasy world, we would work together and get through this. However, deep inside I felt this overwhelming sadness and fear. I started suffering more headaches and infections again. My husband's controlling temperament and jealousy was suffocating but I really thought it was love. He told me he only got angry because he loved me. *Why would I question him?* With being deeply in debt and only one junky car, additional types of stress now evolved. He admitted to me that one of the reasons he wanted to marry me was because he thought all Caucasians visiting Hawaii were rich. (He thought I had money!) My love bubble burst along with my fairytale. I felt like a failure once again.

The party boy and spender that my husband's father warned me about was true. We ate out every meal or joined his parents. With so many bills, a disconnected phone, I immediately got a nursing job, worked full time and carried all the insurance. I enjoyed my job and it became a respite from my real life. My husband, on the other hand, golfed every day and worked part time bartending when they needed him. The only good I felt was that I was away from my past abusers. That felt freeing but I didn't realize I was back in a dysfunctional lifestyle with a different type of control and abuse. I was living in Hawaii. *What more could I want?* So I shut up and put up. Headaches, depression, reoccurring sinus infections and bronchitis plagued me the three and a half years we were there. I was constantly on one antibiotic or another. I also discovered I had severe seafood allergy. One episode resulted in anaphylaxis symptoms. Being so fair skinned, I'd pay the price for a day on the sunny beach. I suffered severe sun stroke that required IVs to get me through second-degree burns on my body.

Unknown to me, my wedding came with "conditions." These "conditions" were made at my wedding between my mother and husband. One of the conditions was if I moved to Hawaii we had to move back to Wisconsin after a couple of years. So as those years passed, my husband got restless. He was not ready to experience life in

Wisconsin, by my family and in my hometown. This eventual return to my hometown was already set in motion. I was reluctant, afraid and devastated to think I would be back where all my past abusers lived. I wanted to forget my past and leave it behind. I dreaded the emotional fear of what would happen when I would see my abusers again and what they would tell my husband.

Once we moved back, my worst fears were realized and the threats returned. I felt like that helpless little girl again. Although I was now a "happily" married woman, I fell right back under their control and spell, and just tried to avoid them at all cost. The threat and fear of my husband finding out was overwhelming. My family never knew of all the abuses and wondered why I wasn't happy to be back "home." The two neighbors and friends that were the abusers were still friends with my family and lived next door. We lived with my parents for five months, just long enough to feel the suffocating presence all the while pretending I was fine. For me, I did not know, nor was I taught, growing up, what boundaries were. I certainly did not know that I was allowed to make boundaries now. Since I never learned coping skills, I lived in fear and anxiety, worrying as to when I would run into these men again. My marriage consisted of me being the doting wife, working full time at a nursing home along with four other part time jobs to keep my husband happy. This allowed him to participate in bowling, billiards, golf, dog track races, card games (yes, gambling), a Goldwing motorcycle with the club membership, eating out and having drinks most nights. To add to my stress and exhaustion, he wanted me by his side watching him have fun and cheering him on. If I walked off to visit or talk to other friends he would threaten me and get so angry he would break things, glasses, slap the wall or whatever he could get his hands on. If he didn't bowl well it was my fault also because I hadn't given him my undivided attention.

I was drowning. This additional abuse caused me to question who I was, again. I was so busy working to support his vices that I felt like I was a puppet. The saddest part of my world was that I thought this was all normal. When my husband's job moved to second shift and I remained on day shift, I could tell the decrease in our time together started to change our marriage. He started talking about other women he worked with, how he would take his breaks with them and even drove me past where they lived. He told me how he talked about intimate topics with them. I was dumb enough to listen. I didn't know what he wanted from me, to scream and get jealous? I only knew he enjoyed his freedom to come and go as he pleased. With me at work, he maintained his lifestyle. I caught him in lies and bills again started piling up. I found out he had taken out 11 charge cards and they were maxed. He got back into gambling and I would find cash advance slips tucked away in drawers and pockets all over the house. When confronted, he became wild with anger. Now, I recognized he was "Peter Pan" and did not want to grow up.

Common sense told me something had to be done and I insisted we go see a counselor. I set up a very tight budget and he became furious that he did not have enough money to continue his past lifestyle. He told our friends I would not give him any money and our friends were becoming divided. Finally agreeing to a counseling appointment, we went. The counselor said it sounded like I was married to a bachelor and he laughed. No goals or return appointment needed. The counselor believed everything my husband said and refused to hear my side. My husband took it as a compliment. I was insulted and discouraged. I requested a different counselor and made another appointment. This time the counselor was realistic and set up some goals and a return appointment in a week. Hubby would not have any part of that. He told me I was the one with problems and he was done with doctors. On the exact day, our 15th wedding anniversary, our marriage and life together ended with him holding a gun threatening me, all because I was insisting on counseling and not giving him any money. He left me and moved in with another women. With all the outstanding bills and legal wheels turning slowly we ended up filing bankruptcy. I got to keep the house minus furnishings. I was completely broke. What was happening to my fairytale?

This is when I feel another stage of my fibro journey began. After the emotional and psychological abuse and fearing for my life at the ending of my first marriage, I became extremely depressed, suffered an emotional breakdown, developed bulimia/anorexia and at a little over 100 lbs I was finally convinced to be admitted for treatment. I was hospitalized for two months followed by extensive ongoing outpatient therapy. As I mentioned at the beginning of my story, my earlier childhood abuses were not uncovered until I was hospitalized and received hypnosis therapy. I had buried all those memories for years. Unbeknownst to me, the buried abuses that happened to me at a young age set me up for later sexual abuse due to lack of understanding boundaries along with threats by abusers if I ever said anything. That in turn opened me up to additional abuses and lack of self-esteem during my adolescent and teenage years. Unfortunately, I was not aware of these past abuses when I got married and aimed to please at a cost of losing my own identity. I found I was married to a narcissistic person who did not know what the word "compromise" or "sharing" meant. The unfolding of all the past traumatic events after the end of that marriage changed me forever. There were several suicide attempts. I felt I could not survive on my own even though I had a good job as a nurse. The lack of self-esteem and finding out that my husband had been straying was devastating. My family was caught in the middle and did not want us to divorce, but they didn't know the whole story.

With all the pressure and divided support of family and friends, my counselor and I felt I could no longer handle my nursing job and I had to quit. I felt my life was over and had no purpose in sight. I did find another job but with no car and having to depend on others for transportation, I was totally humiliated. I was also heavily medicated. Another emotional breakdown was inevitable after being let go from my new job. I was hospitalized, again, for several weeks and then arrangements were made for me to go into transitional housing about 30 miles away to try and get myself back into society. A pastor who had talked to me while in the hospital put me in touch with a local church. I funneled all my time and energy into the church. Looking back, I realized I became excessively involved with a cloistered cult-like religion. I went from one addiction to another.

While attending that church, I thought I had met a good Christian man, and believed him when he said he would "take care of me." After all, I felt like I couldn't take care of myself. Looking back there were definitely red flags. He was 37 years old, never married, never had a long term or intimate relationship with a woman. Red flag no. two, our relationship proceeded *so* fast. We met in June and *everything* we did revolved around the church. His parents wanted to come and see my house and we did set up a time for them to meet my parents as well. He wanted to get married as soon as possible but I wanted to wait for at least a year. However, I thought, *How can I take care of myself?* So out of fear, I gave in. In October we got married. This was definitely a rebound marriage. What I felt was *not* love, but he said he would take care of me. Within months I was pregnant with my first child at 40. I had a new husband that had never grown up, along with a stack of unpaid bills, a wreck of a vehicle and then the job hopping started. My house that survived my first divorce was sold to pay his bills. (Here we go again.) I thought my second husband would be my savior, as he led me to believe. The love I felt was exclusively for our soon to be baby and I threw my heart and soul into raising our beautiful daughter. I suffered from severe post-partem depression and total exhaustion. I was so overwhelmed that all I did was sit and cry in this tiny little apartment. Second hubby was a diabetic and for some reason I was always taking care of him. I was afraid to take my daughter out for walks for fear of something happening to my husband. Here I had this beautiful perfect baby girl and this should have been the happiest time of my life. Instead, I kept stumbling along. I got no help or relief with the baby because my husband said he was too tired from his job and again his diabetes was more important. I was breastfeeding and she turned out to be a three- to four-hour feeder around the clock. Exhaustion consumed me. When she was about a month old, my husband was making tacos and they caught on fire in the toaster. In my rush to grab the baby, I fell injuring my back. The pain was excruciating and consumed my entire back. My husband kept dismissing it, as his diabetes was far more important. We had minimal health insurance. Fast forward to four moves later and hubby was now on his fifth job, I was still suffering with back pain. We finally moved into a cute home and found out once we moved in that it was infested with carpenter ants. After two applications of toxic spray to kill off all the colonies, we were told it was safe to go back in after eight hours. To this day I wonder how safe?

Our daughter was about 18 months old needing regular pediatric checkups. By some miracle, we started seeing a family doctor who specialized in osteopath. He listened and was sincere and started to do adjustments on me and found out I was showing extreme pain on all the pressure points...he called it inflammation of the nerves and I heard the word for the first time, *fibromyalgia*. My doctor was ahead of his time and he believed in and treated me. I was the one who did not know or realize what he was saying or what this syndrome entailed. During that time, I was also working part time evenings at a floral shop and I was being exposed to pesticides the owner sprayed in the connecting greenhouse. I found out later it was approximately every six weeks. One night while working at the shop I got so ill I couldn't breathe. My hands tingled and I felt dizzy. As I left work, I realized that being out in the fresh air helped. The next day I went to see my doctor along with the name of the pesticide used. He told me I was suffering from a chemical induced asthma. If that contributed to my fibro or not I'm not sure, but it definitely was a major health issue. This resulted in quitting that job. Unfortunately, many chemical exposures don't reveal themselves until years later. As for me, I still suffer from asthma since that time. I suffered another flare when exposed to compressed particle board used as a base for a bed mattress, thus causing our daughter to have the same condition of chemical asthma as me. *I wonder did the ant spray contribute as well?* I was hypersensitive to perfume, flowers, smoke, and most scented soaps so my diagnosis started to make sense.

About a year later, we moved away and during the next few years I would go visit this doctor of osteopath twice a year for treatments and his magic touch. The last time I saw him, he said I was in a full flare and could not handle adjustments at that time. This doctor died eight years ago and since that time I have not found another doctor of osteopath who did adjustments or who voiced understanding of my overactive nerves. I was constantly tired, exhausted, depressed, and overwhelmed and suffering from sinus and ear infections. My life was always like a rollercoaster and I was in survival mode. In all, we moved nine times in our first ten years of marriage. The cost was huge not only financially but for our daughter who ended up in different schools and difficulties trying to fit in. She was exhibiting ADD but a private religious elementary school couldn't be bothered with such questions and academically she struggled. At the time, this was my husband's way of keeping us isolated and under his control. The emotional isolation and mental abuse was unending. His job hopping was always someone else's fault and his controlling personality increased and he began to monitor *all* my time. He screened the TV shows I watched and told me the devil was in me if I watched something he didn't approve of or he felt went against the Bible or church teachings. I resumed counseling and planned to separate and get our daughter into counseling as well. I told my husband I don't care where you get help but you have to get into counseling. We did go and see our pastor together several times but he never would go for his individual counseling. His behavior became more controlling and extreme. It was a terribly emotional time and at this same time my father, a co-worker, her husband, and their youngest son all died within days of each other. The co-worker was my daughter's teacher and she was as devastated to lose grandpa and her favorite teacher within days as I was. Four funerals in one week. *How do you heal from that except slowly?*

After a traumatic visit to see her paternal grandmother with her father over Christmas break, our daughter came home from that trip a very different child. She told me he had tried to lose her in the woods up north two times during that week. Later that night, she called me to her room and asked if I could make an appointment for her to see the lady counselor I talked about. An appointment was made for two weeks out and I asked to put her on the waiting list in case there were any cancellations. Her father saw the appointment on the calendar and questioned what that was for. I told him and his bizarre behavior increased. He paced and kept questioning me what was going on. He would creep into the dark bedroom at night and stand over me, bending over close to my face. I pretended to be sleeping yet kept one eye open. Our pastor told him to move out for a cooling off period and he had every excuse in the book why he couldn't and kept stalling. As luck would have it, the counselor had a cancellation and I took our daughter in earlier without her father's knowledge.

Now for the shock of my life. In our daughter's first visit with the counselor, she revealed that her father had sexually abused her along with other mental and emotional abuse. The counselor called me into the room. She looked me in the eyes and told me I had to be strong for my daughter. I walked in the room and she was curled up into a fetal position just sobbing. I was speechless and felt like all the breath had been taken out of my lungs. Our counselor was a Godsend. There was now no turning back and that night we immediately went into a woman's shelter for the next three months while the legal system moved at a snail's pace. No contact was allowed. He told them he did not know why I had him arrested. Yet when he was arrested, he stated to the police, "I wondered how long it would take you to catch up with me." He also admitted he had sexually abused her (but only two times) to both our pastor and the police. His family hired the best lawyer money could buy and our daughter had to go through all the horrible questioning on the stand, mandatory physical exams, and unending interviews. In the end he was given only one year in jail under "Huber Law." He was allowed to leave jail from 6:30 a.m.–7:00 p.m. for work. He didn't have a job, but his family paid for a storefront so he could advertise computer and X-ray machine repair. Knowing her father was still in the area, my daughter had an emotional breakdown. She could not function at school and lost a year of high school and tried numerous times to end her life. She spent six months in day treatment and additional abuses by her father were now remembered. I notified the police but was told that would mean going back to court if we wanted justice. She couldn't handle it.

The overwhelming emotional rollercoaster was nonstop. To this day, I do not know how either of us made it. It feels like a fog and a bad dream. I know I suffered extreme depression and overwhelming exhaustion constantly. Every day I got up, took my daughter to school or treatment, worked a five hour shift, went to appointments, picked her up and fell into bed. Day after day, month after month, year after year. I hurt, I ached, I was exhausted, and had migraines. Housework was unheard of. I isolated myself. Eight years later, my body pain and exhaustion just continued but I kept functioning and working for my daughter. She had threatened to quit school and not graduate. She even made plans to move in with a boy she met online. I knew his parents and we agreed going to the technical school in our town would be better than them living in an apartment miles away. So to keep her from dropping out I had the boyfriend move in with us, separate rooms, *right*, but she stayed in school. A month before she graduated, she told me some things about why she was going to break up with her boyfriend. I evicted him from the house. The next day she had a change of heart and wanted him to move back and I said absolutely not. She was on so much psych medication that I don't know how she could function.

One month before her high school graduation she moved out and in with a girlfriend. She was 18 years old and I had no legal rights. She was so angry at me and stopped communicating. Through all this upheaval, all I wanted for her was to graduate from high school. I wanted to watch her walk across the stage and get her diploma. That had been my driving force and now I wasn't sure that was even going to happen. We had made plans to go shopping for graduation clothes. I had planned a big family graduation party but she wouldn't talk to me. All I could do was cry. I called all the guests and canceled her party. The day before her graduation I had a mental breakdown in my counselor's office and ended up in the hospital. I never got to see her walk across the stage and graduate. It was the one thing I fought so hard for and I didn't get to see it. I was devastated again. Her Godparents came and attended her graduation and visited me at the hospital. They have been my rock and support system to this very day, along with a few close friends and my mother.

Four months later, my daughter moved back home after counseling intervention and remains at this writing. I am happy to say we have healed. Our relationship has resumed, even better to this day. I just kept loving her and telling her that. We truly have survived. She finally started settling down, was working, and enjoyed a small but very close core of friends.

Due to fibro, I retired earlier than planned. I worked part time and my employer started to make demands on me as if I was a full time employee. It took its toll on my health and my fibro flared causing me to be unable to attend all required meetings. I loved my job but the increase in my duties, the pressure I felt from my boss, along with the written warnings, became overwhelming. I decided I had had enough. I gave my two week notice. I had put in ten years at this job, but was ignored the last days I worked. I felt so hurt and sad. It was the best thing I ever did for myself. Now my life consists of accepting that I have a "new normal" when it comes to my health and lifestyle. My lack of energy along with mental fog, depression, unexplained rashes, tactile sensations of needles poking me or wet drops on my skin, chest pain, restless leg syndrome, cold hands and feet, insomnia, irritable bowel syndrome, headaches/migraines, dizziness, vertigo, lack of coordination, bladder and urinary episodes, swelling, stiffness, weight gain, anxiousness, anxiety, heart palpitations, eye sensitivity, eye pain, blurriness, issues with focusing and thinning of retinal nerve fiber layer resulting in difficulty reading and eye strain, dry eyes, and yes, the guilt and frustration of being unable to do things I once did because my mind is willing, but the body is weak. I have been and will continue to be a survivor to the best of my abilities taking one day or moment at a time. My tolerance for any of the usual meds to help treat fibro all gave me severe side effects so I was weaned off of them. I just use over-the-counter pain medication and continue to suffer. I also take vitamins, watch what I eat, and recently started CBD oil. I remain hopeful.

I was feeling so much better about myself I decided I did not want to be alone the rest of my life and ventured out into the online dating world. This was a whole new world for me but after two years I found someone I truly connected with. We both come with a lot of baggage, but I prefer to call it life experiences. Our first date was a turning point for us and we have been together ever since. I was the happy and fun-loving person again with more confidence. I have been with a wonderful gentleman for almost four years. He has been there for me throughout my official diagnosis and remains understanding and encouraging. We are both great communicators and are there for each other. I found my love.

My daughter and I have been through some of the most difficult times of our lives and I worry she has some of the early signs of fibro, however we remain a huge support for each other. The effects of fibro on all body systems are unending. I believe that the traumatic effects of sexual abuse in my formative years set in motion fibro and the trauma of my first divorce was the first stage of my fibro. My doctor from 20 years ago, made the initial diagnosis when few doctors knew, believed or recognized fibro. Along with the extended stress in my life, I feel my body finally reached the breaking point. It was January 2017 when my current general practitioner officially diagnosed me. Along with him, my psychiatrist, counselor and chiropractor all believe and work together to help me be as comfortable and as productive and active as I can be (knowing that there will be days when a flare will limit my function and I may spend days in bed). I am so blessed to have this medical team, along with this wonderful online fibro support group that is always there, no matter what time of day or night. All have been an amazing help and I feel so blessed. I pray that this may help you in your journey as well as provide invaluable documentation for ongoing research. Knowing we have each other keeps me going.

Gentle hugs to all.

Social Security Disability

By Lynn Andrews

Did you ever think you would have to apply for Social Security Disability? I never pictured I would either. In fact, I didn't know anyone that was receiving disability when I was growing up or, for that matter, until I applied. At the age I applied (I knew I was young) I was only 37!

I had to give up a wonderful job. For nine-plus years, I was privileged to work at my last job. It was in my chosen career at a university where I lived. The other staff members were easy to work with. We also employed six students each semester. This was a chance for graphic design students, majoring in the field, to obtain work experience during school and get paid. They learned all the layout specifics, graphics, illustration, and photographic techniques we used including any computer-aided software, design and layout, laminating, and photo development. While staff members consulted, designed, and laid out the larger publications for the university, students assisted with smaller jobs under our supervision. Our department provided services for free to professors and departments on campus. (We only charged for materials.) The campus had a printing department that could print minor jobs and major ones were taken off campus, being bid out for the most reasonable prices.

This amazing job became a part of my past when I realized I was pregnant with my second child. I already had a six-year-old and knew how I should feel when expecting. This time, however, I became very sick—resulting in taking sick leave that extended the entire length of my pregnancy. I did not know the cause of my illness until the baby was born. Apparently, the "Diabetes Test" required of all pregnant women indicated a false negative for me which meant my doctor did not prescribe the needed insulin. My system went crazy when the baby was born (C-section) and the diagnosis was confirmed when we welcomed our 11 lb, 3 oz baby—11 days early. After his birth and a horrendous six months of not sleeping, I stumbled into my doctor's office, begging for sleep medication. He did give me a prescription for a sleep aid but also sent me to a rheumatologist. I was diagnosed with fibromyalgia. Even with the diagnosis, the doctors didn't know how to "treat" me. Many medications were introduced and this is when I learned of my sensitivity to medications. I could tell within a week if any medication was effective or not.

Life continued, taking care of a baby, my then seven-year-old and dealing with my husband being absent often, due to his job. After a year, my husband found a promotion he wanted and was hired, so we moved.

Our relocation was to an area with a very progressive outlook on fibro! I was able to join a swim group designed specifically for this illness. My husband and I were also given the chance to take a class on fibro at the local hospital. We both welcomed the information we learned and I started to gain a sense of my new "normal."

Something still felt "off" and I decided to get all my medical paperwork sorted to figure out what my next step would be to getting better. I worked on organizing the information starting from the day my son was born, July 1, 1999. After two years, it was clear I wasn't going to be able to work a regular job. The severity of the symptoms would ebb and flow—each day was different. The only constant was pain and an inability to sleep. At the suggestion of another fibro swim friend, I started going to her rheumatologist (about one hour away). That doctor suggested I also go to a nearby psychiatrist. I drove the hour to both and have never been in better hands. These two doctors were truly excellent and I was blessed to have found them. The distance was worth the drive, and I was allowed to coordinate appointments, seeing both the same day. I stayed on top of my compiling paperwork from all my doctor visits. I requested doctor notes periodically, filed them by date, included all medications I tried and why they did/did not work, and any alternative therapy information as well. This was key to my filing, once I made that decision.

The rheumatologist appointments were difficult to plan for since they lasted from a half hour to one-and-a-half-hours, depending on any patient's needs. This was an unusual type of doctor compared to any other doctor visits I had experienced. I didn't realize this new rheumatologist was out of my family's medical network and was shocked when I saw one of the first bills. The insurance had been billed, a large portion denied, a co-pay—which I did pay each time and the rest had been crossed out! A large X covered the page and the doctor's signature was written at the bottom with "paid in full." I didn't realize a doctor would ever be so generous and have learned since that she is the only one. She had RA and truly empathized with my pain.

The psychiatrist she suggested was just as good a doctor but was in my network and did expect all payments to be covered. He was worth it though. He worked with my allergies and suggested medications that didn't block my creativity. I began illustrating again. I was diagnosed with other things, like PTSD from my rape when I was 17, and depression and anxiety along with my insomnia. He listened and believed my answers and was compassionate, something that is rare in most doctors. My symptoms were being managed and I was living, although an altered existence to what I had planned, a fairly decent life.

This was when I applied for Disability. I had doctors who genuinely cared, a couple years of their records, and the ability to articulate and fill out the long Social Security forms that come with each new envelope. I was told from the beginning that the "usual" time frame for receiving an approval—if I would get one—was a couple years and three denials. I don't know why that is so. That's just what I was told.

With two excellent doctors in my corner, and my everyday doctors also believing in fibro, I submitted quite the pile of paperwork. With all the combined professional input, I did get approved for Disability in 2004. I had back pay of five years but was told that if I wanted to get the disability approved, I would have to give up that back pay. I believed the attorney that told me that and didn't argue. I became eligible for Medicare, and received a monthly check. What surprised me was that my children received a monthly check as well.

This didn't erase my disappointment for not being able to work or compare financially to my previous household income contribution. I missed work, but receiving disability did help pay the bills.

After the judgement, within months I got my diagnosis of MS. (I was told by my rheumatologist that not only did I develop fibro the day my son was born but also MS.) Amazing. How different my life would have been if I had been treated with insulin!

After my oldest was out of the house and my youngest was in eighth grade my husband had a chance to interview for his ideal job in his home-town. You probably guessed it, we moved again. There was a school that had eighth grade and high school together, so that's where we sent our youngest. I wanted as much consistency for him as possible. There was a bonus...two of his cousins went to this school as well and in his same grade! The move was fairly smooth for hubby and son, but that's where I lost my medical support, so my move was problematic. I have yet to find good doctors here. (We have lived here seven years.) Since moving to this town, I have had an MS relapse and breast cancer. (Both due to mistakes my local doctors made.) I learned, the hard way, to return to my old MS Specialist (three hours away). Unfortunately, my other two "great doctors" had retired, so returning to them was impossible. There are no rheumatologists here that believe in fibro, much less treat it. I am holding out hope for my new psychiatrist, however. He believes in fibro and is trying to work on finding supplements to help my conditions. He is very understanding when working around my allergies and I find this a breath of fresh air!

I would like to list some common misconceptions about Social Security Disability that I had, and I have heard others echo in on-line support groups. The below information is from when I was granted SSD in 2004:

1. The amount of SSD and the chance of getting it approved has *nothing* to do with the amount of education you have.
2. Your doctors *do* weigh in on your case. Their records from appointments include the medications you've tried, the alternative therapies you've tried, the list of symptoms and

other illnesses you have, as well as their recommendations. All are given to the court.

3. Most people do not know that their children, if under 18, also get a monthly check.

4. How long you have worked or how much you have paid into Social Security is not a factor in your approval/denial.

5. Most people don't file until they have exhausted much of their savings. Once you can't afford to go to the appropriate doctors (and obtain medical records and notes for the courts to reference), it's too late. We all have pride, but you are responsible for your own finances. *Do not wait* until you cannot afford to go to your doctors.

6. You can be married and be approved, and you can be unmarried and approved. You can be divorced and remarried and approved.

7. When you become retirement age, you can pick between your *retirement* $ or your *disability* $. You cannot receive both.

8. If you were married for more that ten plus years, then divorced you can still pick between your ex's *retirement* $, your *retirement* $ or your *disability* $.

9. If you are divorced after being married for ten plus years and you are remarried you can only pick between your *retirement* $ or your *disability* $. You cannot pick your ex's retirement because you are not single.

I do believe I was predisposed to getting an illness like fibro. I was raped at 17. Then my first marriage was to an emotionally abusive man. Ten+ years of constant stress over *everything*! Then the pregnancy without being treated with insulin was the item that flipped my switch. I absolutely believe that the chemicals I came in contact with during my education (photo baths, permanent markers, adhesive sprays, protective sprays for illustrations, other chemicals, etc.), and then at various workplaces along with the non-existing ventilation played a huge part in the development as well.

My background seems to consistently fit with all I've learned regarding fibro. The order is always different, but several elements remain the same. Trauma + stress over a long period of time + exposure to chemicals (does not seem to matter the kind, just that these chemicals are not anything your body should come in contact with) + a specific intense incident = fibromyalgia.

This illness predisposes the patient to developing more illnesses and *always* produces trouble sleeping and intense pain. The other symptoms vary by person but you can be sure that their pain has made them very good actors. Most fibro victims cannot be visually identified as suffering from extreme/constant pain because they try so hard to appear "normal," concealing their pain. No one wants to be around a person that has so many issues, so we act "normal." If we cannot pull off our acting, even after resting before, we simply skip the event, activity, lunch, or app't.

I have also learned over the past 20+ years that hearing "You look so good!" actually hurts many patients. We are acting at *every* event. The more we hear the above phrase, the more we realize that our family or friends refuse to look below the surface and acknowledge the truth. They think they are being positive, but hearing "You look so good" focuses on our appearance not our illness. This greeting seems to be the number one welcome that fibromyalgia patients dislike. It makes us feel invalidated and misunderstood. Instead, we ask you to try "it's so good to see you!" This does not set off triggers for us and makes us feel you are genuinely seeing us as a whole person not just our outward appearance. Thank you for reading my view.

Alternative Tips & Tricks

By P.A.H., *Norway*

In an attempt to give you some ideas that book contributors felt gave them more control over fibro, P.A.H. thought of this chart. The book organizer also added some comments from the book support group, P.A.H. and fibro friends. You will also find suggestions and practical tips that can be helpful for daily life between the two charts. Most important first. The first chart lists the information written in chapters. The second chart lists symptoms the contributors experience including 40 symptoms from the questionnaire. Included in the charts: CBD, counseling, diet, exercise, medicine, personal favorites, and therapy.

Advice on Exercise	Helped	No Help	Comments
General Light Exercise (not specified)	III	III	
- Short Walks	IV		
- Stretches/Bands	I		
- Swimming			So helpful!
- Tai Chi	I		
- Yoga	II		
Training in Gym (weights, aerobic)		VI	MS-1
Warm Water Pool Therapy - Some Relief - after MS too sensitive to warmth	II I		Fatigue got worse
Advice on Food			
Cayenne Pepper		II	
Corn/Soy/Heavily Sprayed Fields (with various toxins)	I		Soy - restricted from hormone+ cancer patient's diets
Eliminate Nightshades (potato, tomato, peppers, eggplant)	I		Will reduce inflammation
Ginger (anti-inflammatory)	I		
Low Food Map Diet		I	
No Caffeine		I	If in diet, not after noon
No Gluten In Food - Helps bloating, not fibro	I I	II	On special diet - allergies in food! (I feel better)
No Milk in Food - Helps - Helps for IBS only	I I	III	
No Sugar in Food - Decaf Drinks - "Diet" Drink/"Diet" Food	II II	I I	Sugar equal: - no yeast - less pain Chemicals equal: - higher pain
Organic Food	I		So important if possible

Turmeric - Helps inflammation - Gives heartburn	 II I	I	
Advice on Medicine			
Allergy Testing - Have A Good Allergist!	II		
CBD Oil (cannabis oil/hemp oil) - Medical Marijuana - Using - Want to try	 I II I		 - Anti- inflammation (over time) - Researching
D3 Vitamin	I		Need constant supplements
Good Pharmacist - To help keep you safe from allergies - Medicine/Supplement interactions	I		Get to know your pharmacist personally, they help so much
Have a good Dr or Pain Therapist	V	I	So important!
Have Dr write everything down for you	I		
Heat Packs	I		Winter I
Ice Packs	I		Summer I
Keep Good Dr (even if far away)	I		
Liquid Vitamin B Super Complex	I		
Magnesium	II		
Medicine with Opioids	II	IV	Allergy I
Medicine, Non-Opioid	I	II	
- Anti-Seizure (pain meds)	I		
- Anti-Inflammatory Medicine	II		
- Anxiety	I		
- Cannabis			
- Depression	I		
- Ibuprofen, other over- the-counter meds	II		
- Kratom			Would like to try
- No Medication	II		

ALTERNATIVE TIPS & TRICKS

- Sleep	I		
Natural Factors (tranquil sleep tablets)	I		
Take Someone to Dr with you	I		
Topical Creams/Patches	I		
Weighted Blanket	I		Reduces Anxiety/Pain
Work: - Could Not Work Required Hours - Made to Resign (due to illness) - Work Couldn't/Wouldn't Adjust (to patient's needs)		I I I	
Advice on Support			
Acupuncture		I	Go to a trained Acupuncturist. Do NOT allow electrical stimulation to be added.
Aromatherapy With EO	I		
Be In A Support Group	VI		
Cognitive Behavior Therapy			
Help With Depression	I		
Hypnosis	I		Uncertain (still trying)
Massage	I		Helpful (must be gentle)
Meditation	I		Decreases anxiety/pain
Mindfulness	III	I	Decreases anxiety/pain
Physiotherapy	I	IV	Always
Reflexology	I		Helps all areas of body

Seeing A Professional: - Not Offered - Psychiatrist - Psychologist	I II I		Other Choices: Counselor Clergy Friend/Support Group
Stress Reducing Techniques - General - Learning Through Trial - Meditation - Prayer - Reading	II I I III I		Always the best!
Other Support			
Backpack Style Purse	I		Distributes weight evenly
Be Creative	II		This is my favorite!
Be Your Own Advocate	III		Necessary!
Epsom Salt Bath	I		
Good Bed	I		Sleep Number
Good Fitting Bra (fitted by a specialist)	I		Basic that's necessary
Good Pillow	I		Secret to good sleep
Good Support Shoes/Flat (possible orthotics?)	I		Sandals, clogs, can be a hazard
Heat Blanket/Pad	III		
Keeping A Journal - Caused Worse Depression - In General - Keep A Schedule	 II I II	II	
Learning Which Symptoms Go To Which Illness	I		
Listen To Your Body	I		
Make A Schedule And Stick To It	II	II	Hard to do!
Make Lists Of Accomplishments To Help You Stay Motivated	I		
Make Your Bedroom A Sleep Sanctuary	IV	II	Nothing non-essential
Music	I		Uplifting

On Fibro Fog Days - Notes (to stay on task) - Plans On Whiteboard - Using Alex	IV I I	I	
Pacing	I		Required to balance life!
Personal Time/Hobby/Craft/ Fun Activities/Family Time	VI		Find happiness in your activities in some way
Remove Trip Hazards	I		Often overlooked
Reserve Energy (sit to shower/cook, etc.)	I		I do this with everything
Saying No When You Can't Do Things - Helps for Pain (may feel guilty)	V I		Hard to get used to Helps you gain control
Talk About It - Family/Friends/Spouse - Out Loud Alone (reduce stress) - Religious Community - To Support Group	 II I	III	
Use Hot Water In Bathtub - Difficulties Getting In and Out Of Tub - Helps (in general) - Stopped (due to heat sensitivity)	 V I I	 I I	
Volunteer Your Time	I		Gives perspective
Weather	I		Learn to read your body
Wool Blankets	I		Help morning pain

There are many things that can help a fibro patient get through the day. Suggestions are in order of importance. You will find your own, in time, to add to this list.

1. Make sure you stick to a good sleep schedule (whether you have slept or not). *Sleep is key to everything.* Relax two hours before bed. If not asleep within half an hour, get up, try again after 15 minutes of calming activity. (If this doesn't work, you may need sleep meds.)
2. *Eliminate as much stress as possible* from your life. (Stress *will affect* your sleep.)
3. *Learn to prioritize.* By saying no to items that don't "speak to your soul or passion."
4. *Find shortcuts.* Sit when showering, dry by putting a robe on. Sit when cooking or dishes.
5. *Delegate some* of the household *chores,* so you are not saddled with everything.
6. *Get help* with grocery shopping/other chores.
7. *Use carts, for support, when walking* in any store and whenever possible.
8. *Listen to your body.* If you are tired, rest. If you're hurting, take meds or supplements. If you are feeling better, try to keep moving. Establish an exercise program, no matter how slight. Do not exercise two hours before bed.
9. *If you become oversensitive or overwhelmed find a quiet place to destress.*
10. *Being religious/spiritual/mindful/active in meditation can help* make your day easier. Remember to breathe deeply.
11. *Keep your mind busy.* You will feel less tired/have lower pain when distracted.
12. *Don't wait* until your pain is excruciating *before taking some medicine.*
13. *Volunteer* your time according to your abilities. (Examples: Hospice visitor/sitter, call a shut-in, work on creative projects, help a person in need.)

14. Realize that *people can sympathize but cannot empathize,* they don't feel the pain or symptoms (unless talking to another fibro patient).
15. *Find your passion.* You have been given your passion from above. These are your gifts to the world. Only YOU have these gifts. Respect your qualities and unique abilities. God thought enough of the person you are becoming that he decided the world could not be complete without you!

This alphabetical list includes all personal symptoms. Yes, the symptoms in the questionnaire are married with other illnesses that were brought up by book contributors "in group." The ten most common illnesses/symptoms are in bold. This section is to let you know that our symptoms may vary, overlap, or co-exist with other diseases. You, the reader, a patient, or loved one, need to know you are not alone.

A	
Achilles Tendon	1/48
ADHD	1/48
Allergy/Food Allergies	10/48
Anemia	1/48
Anorexia	1/48
Anxiety	**35/48**
Arthritis	29/48
Asthma	6/48
Auto Accident	14/48
Auto Immune	13/48
B	
Back Problems	**31/48**
Barrett's Esophagus	2/48
Behcets	1/48
Bipolar	1/48
Bladder Problems	24/48

Body Pain	24/48
Bone Pain	9/48
Bulging/Herniated Disc	7/48
Bulimia	1/48
Burning Pain	7/48
C	
Cancer	3/48
Chemical/Toxin Sensitivity	**43/48**
Chiari I Malformation	1/48
Childhood Sicknesses	13/48
Cognitive Dysfunction	1/48
Cold Sensations	6/48
Colitis	2/48
Concussion	8/48
Confusion	1/48
Constipation	7/48
Coordination Problems	1/48
Costochondritis	7/48
Cramps/Spasms	30/48
Cysts/Tumors	4/48
D	
DDD	8/48
Depression	**35/48**
Diabetes/Pre-Diabetes	6/48
Diarrhea	4/48
Digestive Problems	29/48
Diverticulitis	2/48
Dry Eyes/Eye Problems	20/48
Dry Skin	4/48
E	
Ear Problems	4/48
Eczema	2/48
Ehlers Danes	1/48
Emotional Abuse	27/48

Endometriosis	1/48
Exhaustion	**32/48**
Eye Problems	12/48
F	
Fatigue	**37/48**
Fibrocystic breasts	2/48
Fibro Fog	**34/48**
G	
Gallbladder Problems	6/48
Gastric Bleeding	1/48
Gerd	6/48
H	
Hair Loss	5/48
Headaches	**33/48**
Hearing Loss	4/48
Heart Problems	7/48
Hemorrhoids	2/48
High Blood Pressure	7/48
High Cholesterol	4/48
Hives/Itching	23/48
Hot Flashes	3/48
Hypoglycemia	3/48
Hypothyroid	6/48
Hysterectomy	9/48
I	
Infections	16/48
J	
Joint Pain	12/48
K	
Kidney Problems	2/48
L	
Liver Problems/Fatty Liver	3/48
Loss of Appetite	4/48
Lung Problems	1/48

Lupus	5/48
Lymph Nodes	1/48
M	
Melena	1/48
Memory Problems	29/48
Meniere's	2/48
Meningitis	2/48
Migraines	3/48
Mixed Connective Tissue	2/48
Mono	4/48
Mouth Sores	2/48
Muscle Pain	4/48
Myofascial Pain	1/48
N	
Nausea/Vomiting	11/48
Nervousness	2/48
Neuropathy/Nerve Damage	12/48
Numbness/Pins & Needles	10/48
O	
Osteomalacia	1/48
P	
Panic Attacks	4/48
Periodic Immobility	2/48
Physical Abuse	16/48
Plantar Fasciitis	3/48
Polycystic Ovarian Syndrome	1/48
Psoriasis	1/48
PTSD	8/48
R	
Rashes/Blisters	5/48
Raynaud's	1/48
Reflux	5/48
Restless Legs	23/48

S	
Scleroderma	1/48
Seizures	2/48
Sensitive To Light/Sound	3/48
Sensitive To Touch/Clothing	2/48
Sensory Overload	2/48
Sexual Abuse	24/48
Shingles	2/48
Shortness Of Breath	1/48
Sjogren's	4/48
Skin Sensitivities	2/48
Sleep Apnea	17/48
Sleep Problems	30/48
Spastic Colon	2/48
Spine Surgeries	4/48
Stiffness	8/48
Stress	**32/48**
Stroke	4/48
Suicidal	4/48
Swelling Hands/Feet	26/48
T	
Teeth Problems	3/48
Temperature Dysregulation	4/48
Thyroid Problems	13/48
Tick Bite	6/48
Tinnitus	5/48
TMJ	14/48
U	
Ulcers	1/48
Unstable Hormones	16/48
V	
Vertigo	10/48
Vision Loss	1/48
Vision Problems	4/48

Vitamin Problems	5/48
W	
Weak Extremities	7/48
Weight Gain	**32/48**
Weight Loss	11/48

Essential Oils

———— ✐ ————

By Hannah Tanas and Autumn Moulton

Every day you have a choice on the type of impact you want to make on the world around you. Whatever you choose, will make a difference. Let's choose to make that impact positive!

Our Wellness Journeys

The statistics are alarming! There are currently 5,534 hospitals in the US *(AHA 2018)*. Americans are leading shorter and less healthy lives compared to people in other high income countries (Avendano and Kawachi 2014). It has been found a mere five to ten percent of all cancer cases can be attributed to genetic causes. The rest of the cancer cases, it is thought, are linked to diet, lifestyle and environmental factors *(Anand et al. 2008)*. How did we get ourselves to this place? Is there anything we can do to change the odds for our future or that of our families?

My husband and I began to take our health seriously almost four years ago. Up until then we would have considered ourselves pretty average. We tried to eat healthy and bought whole grain bread, ate salads, tried to exercise and did not eat *too* much fast food. We could tell eating healthy made us feel better but didn't really understand why. Around this time a friend introduced me to using essential oils as a way to support our immune system and to help stay above the wellness line. I'll be honest I really didn't think much of essential oils or see the whole value in reducing the toxins in our home. I liked and trusted my friend and thought "what the heck, why not try it?"

Fast forward two to three years. My husband and I sort of dabbled in aromatherapy, began to learn to read the labels on our foods, focused more on the farm to table approach and ditched a whole bunch of *cruddy food* in our cupboards. At this point we thought, "Hey, we're eating mostly organic. We do our green smoothies. We thought we had reached the pinnacle of wellness!"

In our minds, we assumed it didn't really matter what chemicals we were using on our skin or cleaning with because we weren't *consuming* them. It's not like I was making a salad with Windex, 409, or my favorite scented lotion, right? However, according to the Environmental Working Group, adults (on average) apply 126 unique chemicals to their bodies daily! Many of these chemicals have been linked to infertility, respiratory issues, and are *known* carcinogens! *(EWG 2002)*

In time, the evidence continued to mount and we realized that we had to make the jump to going chemical free. Sadly, we have witnessed our family and friends who have felt the disastrous effects of cancer, autoimmune diseases, mental illness, diabetes, heart disease and infertility just to name a few illnesses. We knew there were effective chemical free options for cleaning, to boost our immune systems and strived to live *above* the wellness line. A couple of friends suggested using the Environmental Working Group's website or APP to help us look at what products in our house were safe and which ones needed to be pushed out the door. We started scanning and reading labels and rounded up a large box of shampoos, dish soaps, body lotions, make-up, perfume, baby products and laundry soap all filled with endocrine disruptors, carcinogens and respiratory issue causing substances!

Since discovering all this information, we reopened our original diffuser and essential oils from Young Living. We also purchased a brand new set and dove in! We have replaced our household cleaners with a few microfiber clothes and a bottle of Thieves Cleaner. We now have an arsenal of favorite Young Living oil blends. (There's an oil for everything.) In our home we have Young Living oils for calming down hyper toddlers (Frankincense, Lavender, Cedarwood, and Stress Away are a few top choices in our house) and several oils help us sleep better and boost our immune system. There are oils that improve focus and alertness. Some oils help relax our minds (calm our thoughts). Others support happy moods and lift sad feelings. I could go on and on!

To explain the difference this lifestyle change has made in our family environment and with our health would be hard to put into words. To say we "feel and act healthier" would be an understatement. As I teach essential oil and wellness classes, I often mention to my class that while sharing Young Living Oils may be my livelihood (job), it is also a way I can bless my family. At the end of the day, even if I had NO financial gain, when I see that non-toxic Thieves dish soap sitting on my friend's counter, I know I have changed someone's life for the better. Again, if I see a friend ditch and switch their cosmetics laden with toxic chemicals, sharing my knowledge (because I love them and want them to live a healthy life) helps this individual and their family improve their future above the wellness line! I'm not going to lie and tell you my family never gets sick, but I will say our whole family feels so much better. *Every day!* From more energy, positive emotions, and healthier immune systems, our lives have forever been positively changed. As the gatekeeper to my home, it's my commitment to give our children (the next generation) a life that is full and healthy. (Autumn Moulton)

I'm Hannah (Hammons) Tanas. I was born in Geigertown, PA, but spent most of my growing up years in New York City. I'm a mom of two active young boys and feel very blessed to be their mother. They keep my life full and exciting! I have always loved being in nature, whether it's hiking, gardening, or taking my boys to the park. Some of my favorite treats in life are Indian food and a warm cup of chai.

My family calls me the "canary in the mine." Let me explain:

Since our bodies are organic in nature, meaning carbon-based, it is imperative that we use carbon based (organic) products on our skin, in the air around us and in substances we take internally. Using synthetics (man-made products) causes a buildup of toxins in our body. I have experienced this firsthand as so many do. This is called our "toxic burden" and each person's toxic burden is the level of toxic chemicals they have accumulated in their bodies. This build up is caused (intentionally, or unintentionally) by what we put in, on and around us. Over time this greatly affects our body's natural system and the functions our body automatically needs to run. When filled with toxins, you can imagine how the body begins to break down, how disease can start, and how our body begins to run dysfunctionally. It's a well-known fact that natural, plant based products synthesize in our system, are metabolized by our bodies and can be broken down and excreted. These natural products do not cause any harm or damage to the cells in our body. For this reason, it is important that humans use natural products that our bodies recognize. These earthly ingredients don't accumulate or create toxicity which can lead to all kinds of health problems. Young Living Oils offer this natural solution *and* draw out toxins in our body from past exposure!

When I'm not busy being a mom or outside "soaking up nature"—you'll most likely find me opening a bottle of Young Living Essential Oils or reading an educational article about such essential oils. Young Living Essential Oils have been a *HUGE* game-changer in my life. I was first introduced to Young Living back in 2013 by a friend of mine from college.

She recommended essential oils to me because she knew I struggled with extremely pernicious eczema. After I began using Young Living Essential Oils, I noticed a significant improvement in my symptoms. I began switching all of my personal care products and household cleaning products over to Young Living Products in order to relieve myself of the chemical load my body had been bearing. What a day it was for me! After 17 years of struggling with such severe eczema, I realized I had been eczema free for a whole year! What better firsthand experience could I have seen?

After experiencing the benefits of essential oils in my body, I have been able to see the benefits in my kids as well. Using essential oils gives me an extra tool in my "mom toolbox" that is natural, without adverse side effects. It's so empowering knowing that I can help my boys be the best they can be and positively role model good health.

I was searching Amazon and health food stores for a few years trying to find quality natural solutions to health issues. Everyone claimed to be 100 percent organic and authentic. Upon further research, however, reality smacked me in the face. I found most "natural, 100 percent organic" to be a big, fat lie! USA standards (the FDA puts out there for the stamp of approval) only require essential oils to have ten percent (in some cases five percent) pure oil in each bottle...the rest is *filler* oil, junk and not all safe. The US health care system is another big let down! I turned to Young Living after attending essential oil classes (of other brands) and *not* finding *quality*. Not only is Young Living the oldest essential oil company in the USA, they also own their own farms (across the globe). They are third party tested (to an even higher standard than the French standard of purity). They do *all* the weeding *BY HAND*. The plants are like kings and queens! You would *not believe* the process, even the pest control on all the farms, if you don't see it for yourself! EVERYTHING is done naturally with Young Living Oils including horses working the fields (old school intense quality!) These oils are 100 percent from "the seed to the seal quality essential oils" that work effectively—*ya see, NOT ALL OILS ARE CREATED EQUALLY.* Everyone deserves to know why.

All oils in the world fall into one of four categories: Grade A, Grade B, Grade C, and Grade D.

Grade A: is therapeutic. Made from organically grown plants and distilled at low temperatures.

Grade B: oils are food grade. These may, however, contain synthetics, pesticides, fertilizers, chemical extenders, or carrier oils.

Grade C: is for oils in primarily perfume. These oils often contain adulterating chemicals. They usually use solvents, for example, hexane, to gain a higher yield of oil per harvest. Solvents can be cancerous, and are in most store bought oils. They may also be diluted 80–90 percent with alcohol.

Grade D: is called "floral water." Which is aromatic only and is usually the by-product of Grade A distillation. After all the oils are pulled out, the "leftover trash water" is sold to companies which will fill five percent of a bottle. This "leftover trash water" is put in products and filled the rest of the way with carrier fillers, and label "pure." *This is LEGAL!*

Grade A is the only true pure oil. Grade D would be like walking into your fridge, taking a glass of orange juice and diluting it 95 percent before you drink it! It wouldn't have the full benefits of orange juice. That's why you want Grade A oils. Before you purchase, check to see if the company grows their own plants, owns their own fields, and controls the entire process from "Seed to Seal"—from the farm to the sealed bottle. Pesticides, pollution, previously farmed land—all of it can affect the quality of an oil. Young Living's Oils are Grade A. Why would you go the extra step of using an oil to get away from a chemical—and then use an oil laden with chemicals? It makes no sense. (Average consumers aren't informed on these specifics, and the product producer knows this.)

One of the things that stand out to me is Young Living's "Seed to Seal Process." *It's a promise of integrity.* Gary Young, founder, has said that he never makes an oil for profit. He makes it for a purpose. "Seed to Seal Process" means each plant is hand weeded, there are *no* pesticides used, *no* chemicals, and *no* weed killers. The plants are harvested at their peak. They are then put through a vigorous testing process. Then from the farm directly to your home. The "Seed to Seal Process" is not a slogan. It's a PROMISE! You can learn more by checking out the Young Living story, and fall in love with the company as I have, at seedtoseal.com. This right here is my WHY. (Complete websites listed in Resources and at the end of the chapter.) The videos are really beautiful there and help explain the whole process and why. Please check these out!

I decided to go for quality for my family. The rest is history. Now, almost five years ago…and you would not believe the list of things that have changed in our health since starting Young Living Oils!

Not only are the *oils* amazing but the *diffusers* too! No joke they diffuse the oils at hospital grade level…nothing like anything you can get on Amazon or at Walmart. These diffusers are atomizers and humidifiers that diffuse the essential oils at amazing intensity so you are breathing the best quality oils that can go right into your bloodstream within a minute of even breathing from the diffuser in your room. The effects are instant. Stewardship matters! Quality matters!

Health care matters. *YOU* matter! Can you tell I'm passionate about the process?! :-) Learn more, do better!

It's an honor for me to be a distributor for our company, Young Living. While I know there are other companies that market essential oils, there's a good reason why I back Young Living and why I exclusively partner with Young Living. What draws me to Young Living is their commitment to unequivocal quality, their overriding motto "Seed to Seal," and what it truly means. The Young Living company dedicates their entire energies toward uncompromised stewardship and high quality products from the farm to the factory. You see, I used to live within miles of the Young Living lavender farm in Lehi, Utah. There, I saw firsthand their commitment to quality and their commitment to integrity. They live by what they say. The oils really do go from seed to seal. I'm a witness.

Working with Young Living gives me the daily opportunity to dream bigger, pursue freedom, and live fuller. Due to their life-elevating benefits and because of the values I share with the company, I dedicate my energies and passions toward sharing Young Living essential oils information. I love educating people about their remarkable properties because when you find a good thing, it's hard to keep it to yourself. Let's all pay it forward! (Hannah Tanas)

The Background: What Are Essential Oils?

"Actually, essential oils are 30 to 60 times more potent than herbs." That means they are more powerful and effective than any dried herbs. The reason is that there is only a minute amount of oil in each plant. Remember, that is where the healing power (the living immune system) resides. Therefore, when a cup of tea or a capsule of herb is taken, only a small amount of the healing constituents is made available to the body. On the other hand, when large quantities of plants are processed to distill their essential oils, the result is a much more potent product than even a mound of raw herb. Assuming that all the herb could ever be swallowed.

"It takes a pound of peppermint leaves to yield just a few drops of peppermint oil. Moreover, peppermint has one of the highest yields of all the herbs. Some essential oils like rose oil, require enormous quantities of plant material to yield just a few ounces of oil. A spokeswoman at Young Living Farms told me that one acre of peppermint yields approximately three tons of peppermint herb which in turn yields between 80-120 lbs of peppermint oil. Consider Melissa: "It can take two to three tons of Melissa plant material to produce one pound of Melissa Oil. It takes 5,000 pounds of rose petals to produce approximately one pint (less than a pound) of rose oil. As you can see, essential oils are very potent and just one drop of oil will do more for you than several cups of tea, and far more than a handful of capsules of dried herbs." (Inner Transformations Using Essential Oils, Dr. KeAnne Deardeuff, DC and Dr. David Deardeuff, DC)

Essential oils are not 'snake oil!' Modern science has made amazingly extensive analyses of them to show precisely what makes them work on the molecular level. The chemistry is fully understood and can be clearly demonstrated, as Dr. David Stewart says, "God is in the details!" Organic chemistry is a highly evolved science, and terms such as phenols, monoterpenes, and sesquiterpenes are used to explain why essential oils, extracted from a variety of plant life and distilled to ultra-purity, are so incredibly powerful. Even quantum physics is involved in the scientific demonstration of the unique capabilities of essential oils. This said, not all oil is created equally. Young Living Essential Oils is the only brand that *GUARANTEES* organic oil from "Seed to Seal." No other oil on the market has that guarantee attached to its name. Every step of the process is overseen by third party testers. *No* dilution or alteration! I used to use the cheapest oils I could find from the health food store. Hoping I was making a good alternative health conscious choice. Over time I graduated to other brands. When I finally discovered Young Living the smell and quality alone is unbelievably different. If you smell a lavender oil from another company it does not even smell like organic lavender. "Seed to Seal" is more than important! It is a MUST!

The History of the Young Living Difference

The company was founded by D. Gary Young. In the late 1980s. He began studying essential oils as a part of his discovery of homeopathic remedies in his quest for natural healing. At the time there were no aromatherapy books written in English, though essential oil use had been around for thousands of years. In 1989, Gary grew his first patch of lavender plants and from that he distilled the first 3 ml bottle of essential oil. From there, Young Living was officially incorporated in the state of Utah in 1994.

Why is this company better than other oil companies? Young Living is the world's *leader* in essential oils. Here is a great link to go to and read about their standards: www.youngliving.com (the full link will be in our Resources List) Young Living has existed longer than any other essential oil company in the world today. D. Gary Young, the founder, has spent decades researching essential oils and what they can do to help heal the human body. Young Living owns their farms or partners with farms around the world and has strict standards on the land, the seeds, the harvesting process, and the distillation of the oils. Additionally, they test each batch to make sure that what goes inside the bottles meets the standards for purity and potency and that the chemical constituents are the proper proportions for the oil to be effective. These steps are referred to as their "Seed to Seal" process. No other essential oil company in the world has that guaranteed standard of purity. Other companies don't own their own farms and they don't have distilleries on site. This commitment to quality results in Young Living building distilleries on site, at each farm, so they can monitor what happens to the plants in between. They have a proven process to produce the best quality essential oils in the world. You can learn more about these rigorous standards at www.seedtoseal.com. Young Living carries well over 500 products. They have essential oils, personal care products, children's products, animal care, supplements and nutritional items and even more!

"Young Living is proud to set the standard for essential oil purity and authenticity by carefully monitoring the production of our oils through our unique "Seed to Seal" process. From the time the seed is sourced until the oil is sealed in the bottle, they apply rigorous quality controls to ensure that you receive the essential oils exactly the way nature intended" (seedtoseal.com).

STEP 1: SEED Seeds are carefully selected by experts based on the previous year crop potency and effectiveness.

STEP 2: CULTIVATE Using sustainable methods, our farming practices set the bar worldwide.

STEP 3: DISTILL We are the largest innovator of oil distillation using several proprietary techniques.

STEP 4: TEST We test all oils using our internal labs, and 3rd party testing. Our standards are higher than international standards.

STEP 5: SEAL Each bottle is carefully packaged to ensure a perfect product shipped to you.

Essential Oils FAQ

How Do You Use Essential Oils?

What do you do? Drink the stuff? Put it in your tea? OK, I know sometimes we may feel like total lame ducks trying to navigate it all, so here is an overview of how to use essential oils.

AROMATIC This is the most common use of essential oils because they are essentially aromatic. You can simply open a bottle and take a deep breath and you will get great benefits. You can also rub them on your hands, cup your hands over your nose, and breathe deeply. A more popular way, is to use them in your cold-water diffuser.

TOPICAL Essential oils may be used all over the body. Some body parts are more sensitive than others, so make sure to use a carrier oil. Place a drop into your palm and rub the essential oil on the back of the neck, bottom of the feet, wrists, spine, top of the head, or anywhere there is a need.

INTERNAL Only use pure essential oils that are labeled for consumption from the Young Living Vitality™ line. You may add a drop or two into an empty capsule and top off with a carrier oil, use a drop under your tongue, add a drop to a glass or stainless steel water bottle, or add a drop to honey or another edible item. Advanced use would be to create suppositories (rectal) or pessaries (vaginal). (Content from the VITALITY book by Jen O'Sullivan. Used with permission from the author.)

Can I Ingest Essential Oils?

There are certain essential oils that can be ingested. Refer to the labeling on each bottle. Essential oils can be ingested in a variety of ways. You can drop them in your glass of water, mix and drink. You can also drop some drops in your food while cooking for flavoring such as Dill and Rosemary. Be sure to remember that these oils are potent and you won't need many drops. You can also put drops of them inside clear/empty vegetable capsules. There are many people who have daily regimens who use several essential oils and put them in capsules. People may have a chronic issue they're dealing with or others may just want to incorporate daily use of oils for better health and wellness.

The Benefits Of Diffusing

Cold-water diffusers are essential to any family that wants to promote a healthful environment.

By diffusing you will reap the following positive benefits:

- Supports a more restful sleep
- Supports better daytime focus
- Promotes healthy air quality
- Helps force dust to the floor
- Creates a healthy ionized room
- Creates an uplifting environment

- Helps neutralize odors
- Safer alternative to candles
- Helps to elevate moods
- Promotes better energy

(Content from the VITALITY book by Jen O'Sullivan. Used with permission from the author.)

What Are Carrier Oils?
Carrier oils help dilute an essential oil, and are great for spicy or hot oils. They can be used as bases for lotions and serums. There are dozens of carriers and it is a good idea to try a few to find out which ones you like. Look for organic, cold pressed, pure, and unrefined carrier oils. Some of the most common carrier oils to start out with include:

- V-6™ Vegetable Oil Complex (great for body application)
- Fractionated Coconut (perfect for rollerball use)
- Grapeseed (good for acne prone and combo face skin)
- Coconut (for face cleansing and lower body application)
- Sweet Almond (for face and body)
- Rosehip Seed (for mature skin)
- Jojoba (non-staining, technically a wax, long holding power)

(Content from the VITALITY book by Jen O'Sullivan. Used with permission from the author.)

Citations

AHA Resource Center. (2018). Fast Facts on US Hospitals. Retrieved December 19, 2018, from https://www.aha.org/system/files/2018-02/2018-aha-hospital-fast-facts.pdf

Anand, P at al., (2008, July 15). Cancer is a Preventable Disease that Requires Major Lifestyle Changes. Retrieved December 19, 2018 from https://www.ncbi.nlm.nih.gov/pmc/articles/PMC2515569/

Avendano, M., & Kawachi, I. (2014, March). Why Do Americans Have Shorter Life Expectancy and Worse Health Than Do People in Other High-Income Countries? Retrieved December 19, 2018, from https://www.annualreviews.org/doi/full/10.1146/annurev-publhealth-032013-182411

https://www.ewg.org/skindeep/2004/06/15/exposures-add-up-survey-results/#.WuFGu-jwbrc

https://www.seedtoseal.com/en/seedtoseal

https://www.youngliving.com/en_US/about/index?hpstory=1

CBD/Cannabis/Hemp "Basics"

By Ashley Lang (CBD American Shaman)
& (An Anonymous Organic Cannabis Farmer)
Introduction by Book Organizer

Like most people/patients, we are all uneducated when it comes to Cannabis. We don't know common terms and their descriptions, let alone specifics. This CBD chapter is the starting point or *beginning* of our learning curve.

The questions below will cover basics. These beginning questions/answers can then be taken with us to a more experienced, knowledgeable source (our doctor or local store—that's right, a dispensary). While we would like to, ideally, ask a primary doctor, the truth is they don't know any more than we do. Some doctors may know terms, a few definitions, others may be able to explain their personal experience with cannabis but cannot direct us to how this natural plant will affect their patients. When it comes to advising starting dosages, suggesting types and amounts of cannabis, or how to combine this natural plant with traditional medicine, most doctors are lost. They cannot explain benefits, possible side effects, or refer us to an organic, trustworthy company.

The administration of this book has come up with some general questions that may be helpful to everyone. When researching we talked to an organic cannabis farmer who wanted to remain anonymous. Her chapter was written separate, but in an attempt to make this subject easier to understand, we combined the two into a single chapter. Therefore, all organic information is formatted in (parentheses).

We have all been in the spot of starting a new medication, learning the dosing, side effects, and with our doctor slowly titrating to get to the sweet spot that helps. Individuals react to medicines differently. All patients know nothing will take all the symptoms, especially pain, away. This is a process of learning how to reduce as much as possible without dealing with side effects that become too bothersome. Experience is found through trial and error and the same is true with CBD or Cannabis.

Commonly Asked Questions

Q) What is the difference between Cannabis/Hemp/Marijuana?
Cannabis: Cannabis is the genus that contains the three psychoactive plants—*Cannabis sativa, Cannabis indica* and *Cannabis ruderalis*. Cannabis has higher levels of THC which can give user a "high" feeling. Cannabis is the correct term for describing the psychoactive plant and its products. (It is the whole full-spectrum plant which includes CBD and THC that we refer to.)
Hemp: Hemp is considered to be in the "sativa" family of cannabises technical ancestor. Hemp contains 97–99 percent (CBD) and less than 0.3 percent (THC). Most importantly hemp is not cannabis and has no psychoactive properties. This is where many CBD products like American Shaman's are derived from.
Marijuana: Marijuana is a term formulated back in the 1930s by Harry Anlsinger head of the Federal Bureau of Narcotics and his team at the time to give the medicinal plant, cannabis, a negative public image to help push his pot prohibition bill.

Q) Which one is the medical profession and others interested in, for pain relief?
Medical professionals and those looking for pain relief are often interested in both cannabis and hemp products. CBD is thought to be one of the main cannabinoids responsible for providing pain relief, although THC also has therapeutic properties as well. Although in higher doses THC can cause psychoactive effects for the user. A person looking for pain relief without psychoactive properties or the "high" would turn to hemp, which is bred to lower THC levels.
(This is a question that will vary by individual. Many are not relieved by CBD alone and turn to a product that contains an equal one-to-one ratio of CBD and THC. This ratio tends to balance each other, providing pain relief with a calmer, less "high" feeling.)

Q) What is the third party testing? Does everyone, do it? Is it rare?
Third party testing is when a company sends out their products to an independent lab, for testing which includes: chemical composition, potency, heavy metals, chemicals, molds, pesticides. This type of testing is not rare and any quality company should readily supply these test results to their customers upon request or have them displayed on their website.
(Often bottles will display if a product is organic, allowing you to look the purity up before purchasing.)

Q) Are chemicals, or heavy metals or other toxins a concern when people look at different sites on the web, and try to research what is best to try?
Yes, hemp and cannabis are known as "super absorbers" and easily pick up anything from their environment and the soil in which they are planted. When researching what products to use a consumer should always make sure the company they have chosen readily supplies these test results.
(A cannabis company considered organic, often uses its own land and farm. There are many restrictions including not allowing any crops to be grown on the land for five years before it is suitable for "organic" production. By owning the farm, the company has full control over the production process and can, therefore, eliminate any toxins.)

Q) Is it really true that CBD is legal in all states? Who decides what is legal. The state or federal government?
Yes! As of December 20, 2018, CBD is federally legal with the signing of the Farm Bill by President Trump. Deciding what is legal is where things can get confusing. For example, a state may decide to legalize the use of cannabis on the state level while cannabis use is illegal federally. This gives federal authorities the right to prosecute.
(The recent Rohrabacher-Farr Amendment limits the ability of the federal government from enforcement in medical legal states. It prohibits the Justice Department from prosecuting patients following state medical cannabis laws. Enforcement of the Compassionate Use Act also has helped many.)

Q) Are people who have allergies, like being allergic to molds, unable to try the pain relief?
No people with allergies should still be able to give CBD products a try. Ask questions to the company you are wanting to try, any reputable company should be able to answer any allergy concerns one may have with their products and provide test results for contaminants such as mold.
(This is where purity, organic "clean" farming and third-party testing is mandatory!)

Q) What ways does cannabis come in? To smoke, but what else?
Cannabis comes in many different forms to smoke. Many will be familiar with traditional flower form which can be put in a pipe, bong, vaporizer or joint. Technology has now allowed for extracts as well that can be put in vaporizer devices or pens much like an e-cigarette.
(Other ways cannabis can be consumed include: prescription liquids, capsules, aerosols sprayed into your cheek, lozenges, oils, edibles, oral/dermal sprays, dermal patches, and tinctures. All of which a dispensary would have to educate you on.)

Q) Are there sample sizes people can try?
Yes. Many companies will offer a smaller "sample" size quantity for consumers.

Q) Are there different varieties for different needs?
Yes, each cannabis strain has a different chemical composition of cannabinoids (such as CBD and THC) and terpenes. Therefore, one strain may be great for someone dealing with anxiety and another better for that person who needs pain relief.
(Medical cannabis has too many positives to list. A few include helping with epilepsy, reducing nausea and vomiting during chemotherapy, improving appetites [even in HIV/AIDS] patients, lowering chronic pain, reducing muscle cramps and spasms. All recorded findings have yet to be clinically proven.)

Q) Would the doctor have to prescribe a certain variety for your specific needs, or rely on the dispensary, or someone like yourself, to suggest something?
Generally, for your specific needs a consumer should look for a knowledgeable person or dispensary to help point them in the direction of the right products for their specific needs. Medical cannabis is not something that was taught to the majority of doctors and is a new method of treatment for most.
(Word of caution, especially for those of you that love to research on the web, MOST CBD Oil and other plant derived products are full of false claims and testimonies. If you want to find a quality company, it won't be on the web—unless you want "snake oil"—a term for junk. Seek out an organic, quality company that the dispensary recommends. Then ask questions!)

Q) Since many fibromyalgia patients are beyond being able to work in their jobs, is there a way to keep the costs low. So, patients can use your products as a treatment option?
Yes, we offer a <u>Compassionate Care Program</u> for those in such situations that allows those consumers to receive a 30 percent discount on all products.
(Again, ask! Get a note from your doctor telling of your health symptoms, diseases, and what areas you need help with. For example: chronic pain, anxiety, stress, muscle cramps, migraines, insomnia, concentration.)

Q) Do all products produce a positive drug test result? Which of the products do not?
No, not all products will result in a positive drug test. If a consumer is concerned about drug testing they should look for a CBD isolate or only a product that always asks for lab results to confirm the product they intend to use is truly CBD only and free of THC.
(Another good question! There are CBD products that have a trace of THC that don't pose a problem, just as eating lemon poppyseed can test positive for a drug test. Ask specific questions about specific products you are considering buying. The dispensary expert should know.)

Q) What are the differences between the terms "organic," "100-percent natural," and other terms?
Organic means no toxic chemicals, synthetic herbicides, synthetic pesticides, or chemical fertilizers used in production. It also means that there was no GMOs used in the growing process of the plant. GMO means a plant that is genetically modified from its original state. The certification in hemp production is a long extensive process and is new to the industry. There are only about 200 companies worldwide that are currently certified in hemp production.
(True "organic" has regulations and strict third party testing. Those tests MUST be available to the consumer. Ask the dispensary); 100 percent natural is a term that means there is no artificial ingredients or preservatives. Also, the ingredients are minimally processed. (*But processed, nonetheless.*)

Q) What needs to be done, for a product to be organic and pure? (I know there are a lot of hoops that must be jumped thru.)
This was basically answered in the previous question. The process has to follow those guidelines.
(Look into the state and federal regulations and refer to essential oil—Young Living—high standard to measure by.)

Q) Which doctors can prescribe a medical cannabis card? What conditions and where can we look for what is available in our area. Is it better to get cannabis in your area, or doesn't it matter?
This will vary from state to state. Not every state allows medicinal cannabis at this time. If you are in a state that allows medicinal cannabis, an active licensed medical physician can prescribe you a cannabis card. The licensed physician also has to go through extra qualifications by the state to prescribe cannabis. To find out if you can get medical cannabis in your state, visit your state government website.

Q) Can cannabis/other have an expiration date?
This is a very loaded question. It really depends on a lot of factors. What is the carrier substance? What else is it mixed with? If you have a manufacturers expiration date from those, I would go with that date.

Cannabis flower itself has a date that it starts to degrade after one year. After one year, the potency and cannabinoid content start to degrade. So, it may not necessarily be "bad," it just may be less effective. (First, anything that is not certified "organic," tread lightly. Second, everything has an expiration date. The better the product, the faster it will expire, or be less effective. The carrier is always a concern. Olive oil expires rapidly and is hard to find high quality. So again, ask. Only accept products with an expiration date printed on the product.)

Q) What was your drive to research cannabis for medical conditions?
Everything began for us when my boyfriend hurt his back while serving on a deployment for the military. Popping pills to numb the pain wasn't an option for him. To avoid prescription pain killers, he turned to natural remedies. He began using Turmeric, Kava and CBD oil. I didn't have much pain at that time, but I had extreme anxiety and was on a few different medications for that. So, I said I would use the CBD oil with him to try and find some relief. I am now off all my anxiety medications! After a year and half of getting pain relief and anxiety relief through these avenues, we decided that since this was so successful for us, we wanted to share this wonderful plant with the world! We researched and learned as much as we possibly could. We opened our CBD American Shaman store in November 2018.

Q) What type of studies and research has been done in comparison of organic versus manufactured cannabis use with medical conditions?
As of now, there haven't been many studies, but this is something that I think will start happening now that we have begun to legalize hemp and the cannabis industry.

Q) Do you think medical insurance will cover any cost of your products?
No, medical insurance will never cover the cost of our products however, at some point we could accept payment for HSA cards so that through a recommendation by your doctor, our CBD oil could be covered. (There is also the Compassionate Care Program that allows those customers a 30 percent discount.)

Benefits of Medical Marijuana and Cannabis Oil

Cannabis products with THC varies, where CBD from the hemp plant has .3% or less THC. You receive all the same benefits minus the high psychoactive effect from the cannabis plant.

(This is where many disagree. Clinical trials do not exist to back up any statements, but many people experiencing chronic pain, will find THC more helpful. By balancing the ratio of CBD and THC to 1:1, the CBD should tame down the negative THC side effects while boosting other positives as well.)

After learning so much about Young Living Essential Oils, I understand that Cannabis, while fast growing, is also a fast absorbing plant. That means it soaks up what's in its environment—similar to us! This means truly organic, pure cannabis is all I'm interested in. With several illnesses, multiple MRI's with contrast (containing heavy metals), I'm ready to improve my health by taking something that will make me healthier, eliminating pain, and reversing some of the toxins found in my 'traditional' meds. I hope this path to healthy living can work for you too.

Questionnaire Form

By Jayne Robinson

Dr. Jayne Robinson came up with the idea of comparing our book contributor's symptoms by having each of them complete a questionnaire. The results (referred to as "In Group") show that many of us shared the same symptoms and have experienced similar medical conditions, surgeries, and tragic situations. We decided to offer the same questionnaire to 48 other fibromyalgia patients who were not involved with this book (referred to as "Out of Group.") This shows researchers, book contributors, and others that the, "Out of Group" or Control Group, is very similar to our book contributors answers. The book contributors are a good random selection of the fibro population. It's interesting to see how many similar symptoms we all share. Both groups have the same ratio of male/female participants.

As you can see, all 40 symptoms have been broken up into two graphs, so that you can view the most common and least common symptoms easier. The third graph shows quite a difference in extremes. This is due to the "family" circumstances, and the various diagnosis dates, etc. There is really no way to make this reflect the different answers more clearly. The huge difference in the Age of Onset vs. Age of Diagnosis (dx) is thrown off due to one or two people believing they were born with fibro, or developed symptoms very early on. They never realized, until later in life, that what they were experiencing was an illness.

The subject matter for the bottom of our questionnaire, many felt was too personal. Due to this approximately one-third of all participants, in both groups, left the bottom of the questionnaire blank—with no reason given. *We recommend this third graph and list of information not be used by researchers, as it is not complete.*

The blank questionnaire we all filled out is shown next. The graphs with tabulated results follow.

The tabulation will be of random information that no one can assign to any geographic area, population, age, or specific person, as no names where attached.

LEGEND

> Dark = Contributors to book referred to as 'in group'
> Light = Non-Contributors referred to as 'out of group'

Blank Questionnaire

Please Circle All That Apply

Body Pain	Depression	Exhaustion	Fatigue	Anxiety
Headaches	Sleep Problems	Bladder Issues	Fibro Fog	Eye Disease
Tick Bite	Back Problems	Hives/Itching	Concussions	IBS
Surgeries	Sexual Assault	Auto Accident	Sleep Apnea	Mono
Infections	Weight Gain	Emotional Abuse	Arthritis	TMJ
Hysterectomy	Sickly As A Child	Physical Assault	Stress	Stroke
Weight Loss	Digestive Issues	Memory Problems	Tumors/Cancer	
Restless Legs	Auto Immune	Swelling hands/feet	Cramping/Spasms	
Hashimoto's Thyroiditis & Specifically		Interstitial Cystitis	Unstable Hormones	

Have You Been Exposed To (Please Circle All That Apply)

Toxins/Chemicals/Pesticides:

Home Life/Profession/Farm Life/Advanced Education/Oilfield

Age of Fibro Onset: Age of Fibro Diagnosis:

Other: Male   Female

Your Profession: Highest Level of Education:

Other Family Members That Have Fibromyalgia

Above will help researchers look at pre-existing conditions, exposure to toxins, stress and trauma we have experienced in our lives. This will help in the pursuit of finding a cure and specific, helpful treatment.

Graphs/Summary

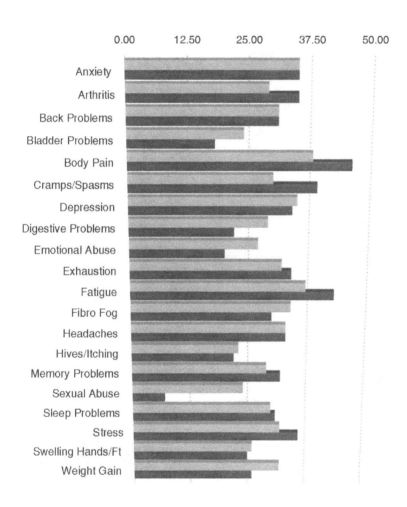

Most Common Symptoms

*Legend and explanation of graphs are on page 229

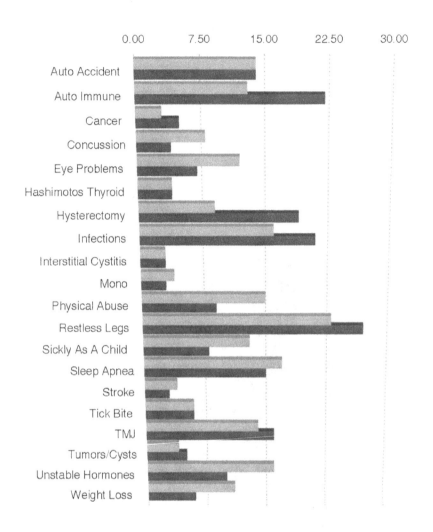

Least Common Symptoms

*Legend and explanation of graphs are on page 229

GRAPHS/SUMMARY

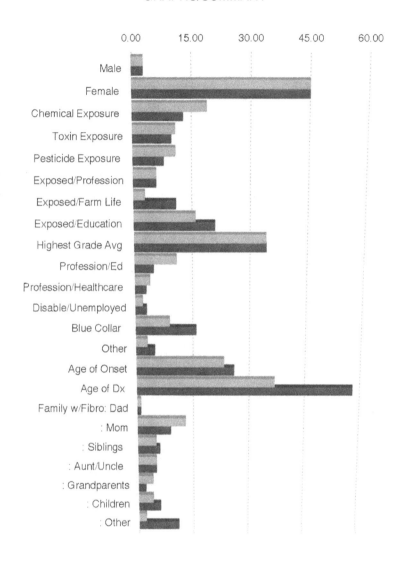

Bottom of Questionnaire

*Legend and explanation of graphs are on page 229

Acknowledgments

Thank you, contributors of the Fibromyalgia Book Edition Group. Whether you helped oversee the organization, writing, editing, marketing, or recruiting of other fibromyalgia members for the purpose of writing a book of advocacy, you have had your hands full. Many followed through with a waiver of liability, questionnaires, financial aspects, and publishing requirements, and these are just a sample of the issues covered while pacifying and helping each contributor. Adjusting deadlines and updating information allowed each contributor to fulfill their chapter obligation with the necessary editing and other additional aspects of the book they took on. Special chapters, contacting experts and resources, as well as time spent working on each section, was met with patience and love. The endless hours required by administrators and the moderator was truly a full-time job and took its toll on each member!

As administration and the moderator look at the group of book contributors, we are so proud of each and every one of you. We were all able to keep communication flowing, in part, because of the various hours each of us kept. One who stays up later, and another who is up early helps the ability to text or talk to the members who live in other parts of the world. While we all have the unfortunate common illness of fibromyalgia, there are many who, for a multitude of reasons, could not complete their desire to be a part of this project. While these reasons are all valid and hard to deal with, we want to acknowledge their true feelings of trying to advocate for more education about our illness and thank them for their efforts. Our hearts and souls go out to all who deal with overflowing plates. This is not an unusual situation and, too often, isn't addressed well by health-care providers.

A special thank you, Tom, for your patience. Your help with our editing, your understanding ways for late dinners, your willingness to live in a dusty home, and my inability to spend much time with you have not been overlooked. My body, mind, and thoughts have been so consumed with this book that I selfishly took time away from our daily routines together. The complaints were few because of your understanding of the importance of this book. Kisses.

The contributors that were able to remain and submit their paperwork, chapter written and edited or photography taken, completing their contribution to the book, left us in awe. The dedication that these members demonstrated by refusing to give up, despite the hardships they continually experienced, was exactly what *will* help all the fibromyalgia patients throughout the world. For the unspoken patients and the rest of us, thank you for your huge hearts!

We were all, originally, members of the first large Fibromyalgia Support Group that went global and grew to a staggering 57,000+ members! One of the special contributors to this book is a microbiologist, Dr. Jayne Robinson. As a patient and group member, her "Science Never Sleeps" letter of support explains the numerous clinical trials currently taking place. Her optimistic vision will help the newly diagnosed, as well as the young fibromyalgia warriors we count among us. Thank you, Jayne, for explaining how bright our future can be.

Other contributors, while not experiencing fibromyalgia personally, work in our behalf. Their dedication to an illness that up to 90 percent of the medical community does not understand or isn't willing to believe is truly moving. How can we thank these doctors for years of research, overtime, and dead ends for an illness their colleagues dispute and harass them about? By advocating for *their* work. And we will! We are honored and accept the burden of spreading the truth and actions of the two pioneer doctors below.

Dr. Bruce Gillis—a graduate of the University of Illinois College of Medicine, the Harvard School of Public Health, and UCLA postgraduate medical training programs—has established EpicGenetics. This company, which, besides offering the FM/a® test for diagnosing fibromyalgia, is presently engaged in research protocols at the University of Illinois College of Medicine. This FM/a® test has since been independently verified, has received a major award regarding its discovery, and carries a test specificity (accuracy) approaching 99 percent (no blood test is 100 percent).

Investigating the potential DNA-related pathways that may serve as the source for the development of fibromyalgia and whether the cytokine deficiencies inherent in fibromyalgia affect COVID-19 infections in patients with fibromyalgia, Dr. Gillis has also commenced a partnership with the Harvard/Massachusetts General Hospital which has received FDA approval to use a vaccine for a clinical treatment trial to reverse the biology of fibromyalgia. The paradigm of what defines the basis and diagnosis of fibromyalgia changed when, in 2008, Dr. Bruce Gillis and a team of researchers in the Department of Pathology at the University of Illinois College of Medicine at Chicago were able to discover and document that fibromyalgia is an actual disease of the body's immune system that exists because peripheral blood mononuclear white blood cells cannot produce normal levels of important chemokine and cytokine proteins which manage the body's inflammation immune system pathways.

Thank you, Dr. Gillis, for "going against the grain" of the establishment and treating fibromyalgia patients with compassion and a helping hand that we so desperately need.

Our second doctor, Dr. William Pridgen, conducts his research in Tuscaloosa, Alabama. He sees his success in his fibromyalgia patients' healing bodies! Dr. Pridgen is one of the most compassionate doctors I know. He will extend himself beyond what is humanly possible to help a fibromyalgia patient in need. This includes phone consultations between patient, your doctor, and himself (if required). The success rate of his treatment for this illness is an amazing 85 percent healthier patients! Humbly dedicating yourself to this illness and helping fibromyalgia patients lead a healthier life is an inspiration to all. Your outstretched arms lend continued hope for so many!

Featuring Dr. Bruce Gillis and Dr. William Pridgen in our book is a remarkable and exciting God-endowed bonus. We are thrilled you have allowed us to be the first patient-advocated book to include your remarkable work! (Information on both these extraordinary doctors is provided in our Resource List.)

We also have an essential oils chapter! (I can't wait to hear everyone's thoughts on this!) We chose the best essential oil company in the business—Young Living! The addition of this chapter will help us look at our lifestyles and review our living practices through a different filter. This will allow us, as patients, to assess our current options and consider how effective they are and how we could try to improve them. Meds are no longer our only option, and they come with quite a price tag of negative side effects! Treating our symptoms more naturally and relying less on meds that don't work well can't be a bad thing. We owe our thankful hearts to Autumn and Hannah for this much needed and useful alternative! Remember, God is in the small details. He has just given some of those details to us.

Since this illness produces constant pain, it only made sense to include a CBD/Cannabis/Hemp chapter, the new stars in everyone's bag of tricks. At the end of the book, a chapter is written by a true CBD American Shaman and an organic farmer! This chapter is a welcome sign for people in pain! Ashley Lang explains the importance of using CBD in natural products and how that can ease pain and other symptoms. Thank you for sharing your knowledge and for being such a compassionate person to those in need. This is a new avenue we have just begun to explore. Cannabis allows us to expand our possible treatment options in ways we never had imagined before.

Our Resource List rounds out the book full circle. Top billing has to go to the Arthritis Foundation. Not only do they diagnose fibromyalgia but they accept us as a member. Rheumatoid Arthritis and fibromyalgia are so close! Nick Turks, director of Health & Support (mid-Atlantic office) has given us his blessing to share our love of his company; Susan Blum's *The Immune System Recovery Plan* is an excellent book to turn to for help with explanations and diet suggestions that have been the reason for my diet change. At my twin sister's insistence, I went to her functional MD and read the mentioned book. Now with the creation of the Blum Center, many more fibromyalgia patients can get help with their entire list of medical issues; Mayo Clinic, how can I even think about creating a book without including you? Mayo Clinic has helped me, personally, in hard times! Their wealth of knowledge is recognized throughout the world. Thank you, Diane Hart, senior manager on behalf of business relations; MyFibroTeam checks in with me through e-mail. They are an interesting, positive way to help handle your daily symptoms.

ACKNOWLEDGMENTS

Elena, thank you for believing this book is worthy of your participation in our resources; _Simple Abundance: A Daybook of Comfort and Joy_ began as a positive daily affirmation that I have shared with many family and friends. The talented author has many books to share. Sarah Ban Breathnach has also graciously allowed us to use her quote for our back cover, and her books you will find helpful in many areas of your life. We are so grateful to have services to go to when we are not strong enough alone, and these are just the tip of the iceberg as many more can be found on websites provided.

Everything included in this book is offered as a service to help, support, educate, and treat fibromyalgia without replacing, but complementing, the medical doctors we see (with the continued prayer that many doctors open their minds and accept the new research and clinical information that is changing the face of fibromyalgia daily). All listed in our resources have been personally contacted and asked to be included because of the positive impact they have had on many of us. I humbly thank each resource for your help and inspiration.

Our publisher, Christian Faith Publishing, fits right in with the personal and professional feelings and experiences of this book. Allowing us to advocate and use all royalties to fund research for this horrible illness so many throughout the world fight. The purpose when taking on this project was to help all fellow fibromyalgia warriors with no want for personal gain. Thank you, Christian Faith Publishing, for believing in us and supporting our mission to make this world a better place. This, I am sure, is the goal of your entire business. You will always hold our heartfelt gratitude!

Through the trials and obstacles that have been thrown at us during the process of writing and publishing this book, I know the only one able to allow _Fibromyalgia: The Invisible Illness, Revealed_ to become a reality was God. Due to His presence and continued help throughout the process, I praise Him through Jesus's name. Amen.

Barbara

Resources

ARTHRITIS FOUNDATION
www.arthritis.org
The Arthritis Foundation is the Champion of Yes. We lead the fight
for the arthritis community through life-changing information
and resources, access to optimal care, advancements in science
and community connections. Our goal is to chart a winning
course and make each day another stride towards a cure.
Helpline: 1-844-572-HELP or helpline@arthritis.org

SUSAN BLUM, MD, MPH
CENTER FOR HEALTH
www.blumhealthmd.com
(link to her books/store/clinic/MasterClasses)
"The Immune System Recovery Plan" by
Dr. Susan Blum, MD, MPH

CBD AMERICAN SHAMAN
cbdamericanshaman.com
(Worldwide wellness through unite-concentrated
terpene rich CBD/Hemp oils and products)
855-427-7386
ASHLEY LANG
Owner
Sun Prairie American Shaman
2687 Windsor St
Sun Prairie, WI 53590
608-617-4849
www.sunprairieamericanshaman.com

DR. BRUCE GILLIS, MD, MPH
EpicGenetics, Inc.
www.fmtest.com
The developer of the **FM/a® Test** for Diagnosing Fibromyalgia
American Association for Clinical Chemistry Award for
Outstanding Research in Clinical and Diagnostic Immunology
'Campaign 250 for Identifying Potential Genomic
Markers associated with Fibromyalgia
and FDA-Approved Clinical Treatment Trial'
Los Angeles, CA.
310-268-1001

MAYO CLINIC
www.mayoclinic.org

MY FIBRO TEAM
www.MyFibroTeam.com
(A Social Networking for those living with Fibromyalgia)
Daily inspiration/check-in/other information

DR. WILLIAM PRIDGEN, MD, FACS
tuscaloosasurgery.com
innovativemedconcepts.com
205-310-7780
Will work with individuals, or with your
current doctor (if unable to travel).
Fibromyalgia patients have an 85% success
rate in improving their health!

SARAH BAN BREATHNACH
"A Man's Journal to Simple Abundance" (50 Essays written by Men)
"Simple Abundance; A Daybook of Comfort and Joy"
"Something More; Excavating Your Authentic Self"
(The Workbook Companion to Simple Abundance)

YOUNG LIVING ESSENTIAL OILS
www.youngliving.com/en_US
Therapeutic Grade A Essential Oils
World's Leader in Essential Oils with "Seed to Seal" Promise
(Other home products: Whole Body
Supplements, Plant-based Cleaner,
Personal Care, Bath and Body, Children's Line and more!)
801-418-8900
800-371-3515 (orders)
www.daybreakoils.com
AUTUMN MOULTON

CPSIA information can be obtained
at www.ICGtesting.com
Printed in the USA
BVHW082059150222
629079BV00003BA/164

9 781638 440307